Live Fully, Laugh Often

...and Don't Forget To Let the Cats Out!

ROBERT STRAND

Evergreen
PRESS

Mobile, AL

ISBN 978-1-58169-429-1
For Worldwide Distribution
Printed in the U.S.A.
Evergreen Press
P.O. Box 191540 • Mobile, AL 36619
800-367-8203

Contents

"Grandma, How Old Are You?"   1

It's Okay To Get Older but Don't Get Old!   5

Grandchildren Still Say the Funniest Things...   10

Even Tombstones Can Tickle the Funny Bone!   17

God Rest Ye Merry Clergy Persons   26

Politicians and Their Parties   37

Happiness and Joy   42

A Church Can Be a Very Funny Place   48

A Blooper Is a Stupid Mistake...   57

Dumb, Dumber, and Dumbest...   63

When God Created Grandchildren...   70

Old Age Is Definitely Not for Wimps   73

Jokes From Around the World   81

Football-Speak Theology   89

From the Wild, Wild World of Sports   93

Just More Jokes for the Fun of It   100

Momma Don't 'Low No Ethic Jokes Here   108

Out of the Mouths of Grandbabes   115

The Best Is Yet To Come!   121

And Now for the Pun of It!   128

A Few "Zingers" To Make Your Day   135

The Church Is Still a Very Funny Place   138

Ever Have an Accident, Make a Mistake, or Misspeak?   145

"Help, I've fallen, and I think
I broke my funny bone!"

Introduction
...and a Bit More

In years gone by, Art Linkletter entertained all of us with his groundbreaking television programs *People Are Funny* and *Kids Say the Darndest Things*. People are still funny and kids still are a delight. So the more things change, the more they stay the same. Some college professor who had too much time on his hands made a study with government grant money (really our taxes confiscated from us). After much research, he declared that "humor tends to recycle itself every seventeen years." So if you've heard any of these jokes or stories before...just smile and enjoy!

The greatest humor in all the world happens when people are simply being people! Life is full of humor for those who look for it! And let's set the record straight at the beginning—our humanness and humor is a delight to God who, through the wisest man who ever lived, penned these profound words: "A cheerful heart is good medicine!" (Proverbs 17:22 NIV) Try it...you might like it! There was also a songwriter who wrote, "A spoonful of sugar helps the medicine go down..."

Now for the question: Is it "spiritual" or "religious" to laugh and be joyful? How about letting the Bible speak for itself? The word *rejoice* or some form of it is written 248 times; the words *joy, joyfully,* and *joyful* appear more than 200 times; the word laugh can be found forty times in the Bible. To be joyful is an attitude, a mindset, and a discipline. How can you be depressed while laughing?

I know, life has become sort of grim, and we can probably remember a more joyful time in the past. Consider this...a study indicates that kids laugh an average of 150 times per day but adults only about ten times a day! What has happened to us? We have a "laughter famine" in this world, but especially in the religious/church world! Somewhere between childhood innocence and adulthood, life has become a sobering reality. When did a well-exercised sense of humor and joy get sacrificed on the altar of adulthood? Who says that being an adult as well as a Christian means that you must go through the rest of your life with a long face and joyless living? Not me! Not you!

Do you need strength? It's in joy! Do you need a physical makeover or an attitude checkup from your neck up? The cure is found in joy! Do you need to celebrate? Release it in joy! Do you hurt? A full recovery is found in joy! Enjoy life! Laugh a lot! In fact, laugh a whole lot more! Give yourself permission to laugh!

Whatever problems Adam and Eve had in days of yore...
Whenever either cracked a joke,
It was never said by them,
"I've heard that one before!"
Enjoy!
—*Bob Strand, 2012*

P.S. It's a proven fact that animals can help bring joy to our lives. Many of our friends have added a cat to their household as they have gotten older since cats are easy maintenance. As a salute to them, we have added a little cat humor at the end of each section so we won't forget to let the cats out...

"Grandma, How Old Are You?"

A grandmother and her precocious ten-year-old grand-daughter were spending the rest of the day and overnight together. Grandma was the babysitter while Mom and Dad were on a short overnight trip.

When it was time to prepare dinner together, the grand-daughter joined in with the food preparations, and a special casserole was placed in the oven for forty-five minutes. While Grandma continued with other meal preparations, her grand-daughter suddenly asked, "Grandma, how old are you?"

The woman was a bit startled, but knowing her grand-daughter's quick little mind, she wasn't shocked. Grandma replied, "Well...honey, when you are my age, you don't share your age with anybody."

"Grandma...aww, go ahead and tell me. I won't tell anybody else."

"No, dear, I never tell anyone my age."

That seemed to satisfy her youthful curiosity. Grandma then went back to fixing their dinner. After a little while she realized the little darling had been missing for about twenty minutes. Much, much too long! So Grandma quickly wiped her hands on the towel and began her search, calling for the girl. She looked all around downstairs, and not finding her,

Grandma made her way upstairs, wondering what her grand-daughter was up to.

There she was in Grandma's bedroom. Granddaughter had dumped all the contents of Grandma's purse on top of her bed and was sitting cross-legged in the middle of the mess, holding her grandmother's driver's license in both of her hands.

When their eyes met, the child loudly announced, "Grandma, you are seventy-six years old!"

"Why, yes, I am. How did you know that?"

"I found the date of your birthday here on your driver's license, and I subtracted that year from this year...so you are seventy-six!"

"That's right, sweetheart. You are a smart little girl. Your grandmother is seventy-six."

"Thank you, Grandma," the reply came with a bit of embarrassment and a sigh of relief because it didn't appear as though Grandma would scold her.

"Well, let's put all this back in my purse and go downstairs. Dinner should be about ready."

They began gathering up the items the little girl had strewn over the bed. The little darling took one last look at Grandma's driver license and then added, "Grandma...it says you also made an F in sex!"

How Laughter Saved the Day

The late Grady Nutt, preacher/writer/stand-up comedian, often told this story about a young family who decided to invite the newly appointed pastor and spouse at their church to be guests at a Sunday dinner. The story goes something like this:

The mother was concerned that this would be a "perfect" social occasion, a perfect dinner that would be a blessing to their new pastor and his spouse. She drilled her two children days in advance about the proper behavior at the table, which fork to use and when, where to place the butter knife, how and when to use the napkin, and so forth. She meticulously planned the menu and spent a lot of time in preparations.

Finally Sunday arrived. The meal was prepared and ready to be served. All were invited to come into the dining room where the beautiful table was set with a white lace tablecloth, their best china and silverware, candles, and fresh flowers arranged perfectly in the centerpiece.

They took their chairs at the formal table where the name plates indicated where each one was to sit. The father of the home prayed the blessing, and when he had pronounced the final "amen," the little nine-year-old daughter reached for her glass of iced tea and accidentally knocked it over! The little brother jumped to get out of the way of the spill and knocked his glass of tea over too! There was a pregnant, awkward moment of silence as everybody looked to the mother, realizing how disappointed she must be. She had gone to all this fuss and effort, and now there was a huge and spreading stain of iced tea and ice cubes in the middle of the imported white lace linen tablecloth!

Before anyone could say anything, the father flipped over his glass of tea and started to laugh! The preacher caught on, tipped over his tea, and he too began to laugh. And now everybody looked at the mother, who, finally with an expression of resignation, picked up her glass and just dumped it out in the middle of the table. Everybody around the ruined table setting roared with laughter!

Then the father looked down at his nine-year-old daughter, seated right beside him, and winked at her. As she in turn laughed embarrassingly, she looked up, almost worshipfully, at a dad who loved her enough to be sensitive to save her from one of life's most embarrassing moments. She winked back. But as she did, that wink flicked a tear out of her eye, and it rolled down her cheek!

Also that day they offered great sacrifices, and rejoiced, for God had made them rejoice with great joy; the women and the children also rejoiced, so that the joy of Jerusalem was heard afar off! (Nehemiah 12:43)

BUT SERIOUSLY FOLKS: Bernard Shaw wrote: "When a thing is funny, search it for a hidden truth." Let's begin right here in this first chapter with a new habit. Take Mr. Shaw's advice and look for hidden truth. Hopefully, most of what you will read in this book will be humorously hiding a nugget of truth.

And here's our first salute to cat lovers:

LET THE CATS OUT...
Cat bumper sticker: Cats might be man's best friend, but they'll never admit it.

It's Okay to Get Older but Don't Get Old!

An older couple was watching television when the husband said, "I'm going to the kitchen for a Coke."

The wife asked, "While you're up, please get me some ice cream."

When he replied that he would, she admonished, "You'd better write it down."

He said, "No, I can remember that."

She added, "With chocolate sauce and a cherry on top. Write it down!"

"No, I can remember."

He was gone quite a while and returned with a plate of bacon and eggs in each hand.

She took one look and said, "I knew you should have written it down; you forgot the toast!"

The five "B's" of old age are: baldness, bursitis, bifocals, bulges, and bunions!

Frequent naps prevent old age, especially if taken while in the act of driving!

Old age: When the gleam in your eye is just the sun on your trifocals.

—

Bob Hope said this on his TV show: "Today my heart beat 103,360 times, my blood traveled 168 million miles, I breathed 23,400 times, I inhaled 438 cubic feet of air, I ate 3 pounds of food, drank 2.9 pounds of liquid, I perspired 1.43 pints, I gave off 85.3 degrees of heat, I generated 450 tons of energy, I spoke 4,800 words, I moved 750 major muscles, my nails grew .00056 inches, my hair grew .012714 inches, and I exercised 7 million brain cells. No wonder I'm tired!"

—

When a tropical storm blew up and caught a cruise ship at sea, a young woman who was leaning against the ship's rail lost her balance and was thrown overboard. Immediately, another figure plunged into the waves beside her and held her up until a lifeboat rescued them. To everyone's astonishment the hero was the oldest man on the cruise—an octogenarian. That evening he was given a party in honor of his bravery. "Speech! Speech! Speech!" the other passengers shouted.

The old gentleman slowly rose and looked around at the enthusiastic gathering. "There's just one thing I'd like to know," he said testily with anger. "Who pushed me?"

—

Several elderly church members were being asked the secret of their longevity. "And why do you think God has permitted you to reach the age of ninety-two?" one sweet little blue-haired lady was asked. Without hesitation she responded, "To test the patience of my relatives!"

One senior husband found the key to safe driving for his wife. He reminded her that if she had an accident, the newspapers would print her age with the police report.

~

Three retirees, each with hearing loss, were taking a walk one fine March day. One remarked, "Windy, ain't it?"
"No," the second replied. "It's Thursday."
The third chimed in, "So am I. Let's have a sweet tea."

~

Albert Einstein, one of the world's greatest scientists, was also known as the original absentminded professor. He boarded a train and was unable to produce his ticket for the conductor. The conductor said, "I recognize you, take it easy; you'll find it." Later the conductor returned and Einstein was still looking. He said, "Dr. Einstein, forget about it. I know you bought a ticket."
"You're very kind," said Einstein, "but I must find it. Otherwise I won't know where I'm going."

~

A group of seniors at an assisted living home were having a good old time discussing their various aches, pains, and ills. Some had arthritis, another indigestion, one had ulcers, insomnia, and on it went. Finally, an eighty-seven-year-old man said, "Think of it this way, my friends. It just proves that old age isn't for sissies!"

~

A family was celebrating an aunt's one-hundredth birthday. Her pastor came, among others, to offer his congratulations. Later, the pastor replied, "Her mind was keenly alert. When I came, she was leading the celebration!"

A local reporter was also there to interview her. He directed a question to this high-spirited, one-hundred-year-old woman. "Do you have any children?"

She replied without hesitation, "Not yet!"

You can forget all about jet planes, race cars, and speed boats. There is nothing as fast as middle age!

Though the fig tree may not blossom, nor fruit be on the vines; though the labor of the olive may fail, and the fields yield no food; though the flock may be cut off from the fold, and there be no herd in the stalls—yet I will rejoice in the Lord, I will joy in the God of my salvation (Habakkuk 3:17-18).

BUT SERIOUSLY FOLKS: Can you imagine that God might laugh? Well, how about this? "He who sits in the heavens shall laugh" (Psalm 2:4). Nor was Jesus Christ, God's only begotten Son, cut from black cloth either. No matter how the Pharisees may have seen Him, the Gospels present Him as a warm friend, full of laughter, a man filled with joy no matter His life situation, who went about doing good and sharing Good News!

LET THE CATS OUT...
"No matter how much cats fight, there always seems to be plenty of kittens." *—Abraham Lincoln*

Grandchildren Still Say the Funniest Things Because They Belong to Us!

A grandfather was teaching his grandson what a real Christian should be like. When the lesson was over, the grandpa got a shot to the heart he never forgot. The little boy asked, "Grandpa, have I ever met one of these Christians?"

A kindergarten Sunday school teacher had her class draw a nativity scene. One youngster had done a nice job in drawing the baby in a manger, with Mary and Joseph and the animals, but the teacher also noticed with anxiety that he had drawn a little fat man right beside the manger. She asked, "Timmy, that isn't Santa, is it?"

Jimmy answered indignantly, "Of course not. That's Round John Virgin!"

He Gets Letters...

Dear God,

Do You get Your angels to do all the work? Mommy says we are her angels, and we have to do everything.

Love, Maria

Dear God,

When You started the earth and put people there and all the animals and grass and the stars, did You get very tired? I have a lot of other questions too.

Very truly yours, Sherman

And then there's the twelve-year-old son's first letter home from summer camp, which read:

Dear Mom,

Send food. All they serve here is breakfast, lunch, and supper.

Your hungry son, Jacob

"An anecdote is a tale," said the teacher. "Now, Sidney, use it in a sentence."

Sidney replied, "I tied a tin can to the dog's anecdote."

One of the mysteries of life is how the boy who you weren't sure was good enough to marry your daughter can be the father of the smartest grandchild in the world!

A lady who ran a nursery school was delivering a vanload of kids home one day when a fire truck zoomed past. Sitting up on the front seat was a Dalmatian. The kids immediately fell to discussing the dog's duties.

"They use him to keep the crowds back," said one five-year-old.

"No," said another, "he's just for good luck."

The third child brought the argument to an end: "They use the dog," he said firmly, "to find the fire hydrant!"

A lady lost her purse in the bustle of Christmas shopping. It was found by an honest little boy and returned to her.

Looking in her purse, she commented, "That's funny. When I lost my bag there was a twenty-dollar bill in it. Now there are two five-dollar bills and ten one-dollar bills."

The quick-thinking little boy replied, "That's right, lady. The last time I found a lady's purse, she didn't have any change to use for a reward."

—

Mother: "Did you thank Mrs. Jones for the lovely birthday party she gave?"

Tommy: "No, Momma. The girl leaving just before me thanked her, and Mrs. Jones said, 'Don't mention it'...so I didn't."

—

Poor Adam and Eve, they had another claim to fame: They were the first ever to raise a little Cain.

—

A small child with a bad cold was taken by her parents to the urgent care clinic. A nurse, examining the child's lungs with a stethoscope, said, "I have to see if Barney is in there."

"I have Jesus in my heart," said the child. "Barney is on my underwear."

—

Laughter in the House

On Palm Sunday, I took my three-year-old grandchild to church. When the ushers walked down the aisle with armloads of palms to distribute to the worshipers, Mikey shouted out, "Oh boy, corn on the cob!"

A Sunday school teacher asked the children just before she dismissed them to go to big church, "And why is it necessary to be quiet in church?"

Connie replied, "Because people are sleeping."

One of the mothers at Saint John's Evangelical Lutheran Church in Lewistown, Pennsylvania, happened to drive by the home of Pastor Gerald A. Krum while he was mowing his lawn. Her six-year-old daughter stared out the car window in open-mouthed amazement.

"Isn't that Pastor Krum mowing the grass?" she asked.

"Yes, her mother said. "What's wrong with that?"

"I thought he could just ask God not to make it grow," she answered.

The Sunday school teacher was telling the little children in her class that God loved them all the time, even when they were grumpy.

"And Happy!" exclaimed Josh, adding, "...and Sleepy and Dopey and Sneezy and Doc and Bashful!"

A little girl, after church, was telling her mother that they talked about Jesus going up to heaven and that He was now sitting with God. The mother noticed a picture of a rainbow and said, "Look at that beautiful rainbow God painted for us."

The little girl replied, "And just think, Mommy, God did it all with His left hand."

The mother asked, "What do you mean? Can't God use both His hands?"

"Of course not, Mommy. My Sunday school teacher said that Jesus is sitting on His right hand."

A family began attending church for the first time, and the kids loved it, especially the singing and communion service.

One day the babysitter was watching the children and fixed them a lunch of burritos and apple juice, a favorite lunch. She overheard the four-year-old, Alisha, begin to celebrate communion with her lunch items. She seemed to have almost memorized the words, except when it came to the cup. She was heard to say, "And Jesus took the cup and He blessed it, and He gave God thanks for it, and He said, 'Fill it with Folgers and wake 'em up!'"

Now that's a pretty interesting theology!

If I Had It to Live Over Again

This wonderful little piece of creative writing has no known author; it's simply anonymous. However, on doing a bit more of research, it can possibly be traced to an unknown Friar in a remote Nebraska monastery. Whatever, it's an enjoyable read that should cause all of us to do some serious thinking about our uptight style of living. Hope you have a chuckle or two as you read this!

If I had my life to live over again...
I'd try to make more mistakes next time.
I would relax,
I would limber up,
I would be sillier than I have been on this trip.
I know of few things I would take seriously.
I would take more trips.
I would be crazier.
I would climb more mountains,
    swim more rivers,
        and watch more sunsets.
I would do more walking and looking.
I would eat more ice cream and less beans.
I would have more actual troubles,
    and fewer imaginary ones.
You see,
I'm one of those people who lives life
    prophylactically and sensibly
        hour after hour, day after day.
Oh, I've had my moments.
But if I had to do it over again,
I'd have more of them!

In fact,
I'd try to have nothing else, just moments,
    one after another,
        instead of living so many years ahead each day.
I've been one of those people
    who never go anywhere without a thermometer,
        a hot water bottle,
           a gargle,
              a raincoat,
                an aspirin,
                  and a parachute.

If I had my life to live over I would start barefooted
    earlier in the spring
        and stay that way later in the fall.
I would ride on more merry-go-rounds.
I'd pick more daisies.
I'd laugh a whole lot more!

The thief does not come except to steal, and to kill, and to destroy. I have come that they may have life, and that they may have it more abundantly (John 10:10).

BUT SERIOUSLY FOLKS: Eleanor Doan wrote: "Since there is but a brief span between birth and death, learn to enjoy the span!" Point well taken.

LET THE CATS OUT…
One sign you have become a cat person:
You'd rather watch an infomercial than disturb Felix, who's sleeping on the remote.

Even Tombstones Can Tickle the Funny Bone!

For most of us, cemeteries are not happy places to be, but then it really depends on your perspective: above it all or six feet under. In reality a tombstone can say good things about a person when they are down, but on the other hand the chiseled message can be funny!

An old lady went to a tombstone-cutter's office to order a memorial stone for her late husband's grave. After explaining that all she wanted was a small one with no frills, she told him to put this message on the stone: "To my husband," in a suitable place. When the finished stone was set in place, she saw to her horror, this inscription:
"TO MY HUSBAND...IN A SUITABLE PLACE."

On a tombstone in Scotland:
John Carnegie lies here,
Descended from Adam and Eve;
If any can boast of a pedigree higher,
He will willingly give them leave.

On the tombstone of a hypochondriac:
I told you I was really sick!

In honor of a person with no name:
Here I lie, and no wonder I'm dead,
For the wheel of a wagon went over my head!

In a New Hampshire churchyard:
To all my friends I bid adieu,
A more sudden death you never knew.
As I was leading the old mare to drink
She kicked, and killed me quicker
Than you could think!

When an elderly spinster died, her family could not come up with a suitable epitaph for her gravestone until one of the family remembered that a cousin was a newspaper writer, a sportswriter to be exact, and asked him to compose the inscription. He wrote:
Here lie the bones of Mary Jones
Her life knew no terrors.
Born an old maid, died an old maid
No runs, no hits, no errors!

About Mr. Foote:
Here lies one Foote, whose death may thousands save,
For death hath now one foot within the grave.

An answer to an epitaph:
As you are now,
So once was I,
And as I am now, so must you be.
Prepare yourself to follow me.

Beneath this epitaph, some living wit wrote in crayon:

To follow you, I'm not content,
Until I learn which way you went!

What's Behind Those Pearly Gates?

A banker approaches the Pearly Gates sweating and struggling with a heavy suitcase. Saint Peter greets him and says, "Set the suitcase down out there and come on in."

"No way!" barks the banker. "I have to bring it in!"

"What could possibly be in there that's so important?" asks Peter. "Open it up!"

The banker opens the suitcase to reveal fifty solid gold bricks. Peter's jaw drops.

"I can't believe that you brought along pavement!"

The young beginning pastor was emphasizing his point at the funeral of an elder who had served the church for many years.

"This man in the casket is just a mere shell." He paused for effect, then said, "The real nut is in heaven!"

The preacher had just finished preaching a stirring evangelistic message titled: "Hell, Where Is It?"

The soloist stood to sing the planned closing benediction: "Tell Mother, I'll be there."

A father was trying to comfort his six-year-old son after their dog was killed by a car with a drunk driver.

"Johnny, remember that Tippy is up in heaven now with God!"

Johnny replied, "But Daddy, what in the world would God want with a dead, smashed dog?"

⌐

Three doctors died, went to heaven, and met Saint Peter at the gates. Saint Peter asked the first doctor why he thought he deserved to enter.

"I was a doctor with the Christian Medical and Dental Society," this physician replied. "Every year I went to the Southwest for three weeks and treated the poor Native Americans free of charge."

"Welcome," said Saint Peter. He asked the second doctor, "And what did you do?"

"I was a medical missionary in Africa for eleven years," she replied.

"Enter into the joy of the Lord," Saint Peter said. He turned to the third doctor and asked, "What did you do?"

"I was a doctor at an HMO."

"Come on in," Saint Peter said. "But you can only stay for three days."

⌐

A man died and went to heaven. An angel escorted him past mansion after mansion after dazzling mansion until they came to a little back lot with a dilapidated, run-down shack at the end of the street. The angel said, "Welcome to your heavenly home."

The man was stunned and said, "Why am I stuck with this run-down piece of junk when all these other people have mansions?"

"Well, sir," replied the angel, "we did the best we could with what little you sent up here."

In the middle of a long-winded sermon, a small child was overheard asking his mother in a whisper that could be heard for several pews around them: "Mommy, are you sure this is the only way we can get to heaven?"

When Sherlock Holmes, the great British detective, arrived in heaven, Saint Peter said to him, "Can you help us solve a mystery? You see, Adam and Eve have been missing for the past several thousand years. Can you find them?"

Sherlock began his investigation and after several days, he returned and told Saint Peter: "I found them over there by that gate." And he pointed them out.

"Well, how in the name of heaven did you recognize them?"

"Elementary, my dear Saint Peter," Sherlock replied. "They are the only two up here who have no navels."

Saint Francis and Saint Peter were playing golf. At the end of the first six holes, each had six holes-in-one.

Finally Saint Peter said, "Look, let's forget about these miracles and just play golf."

A Cardinal and a U.S. Senator arrived in heaven at the same time. The cardinal was given the key to a very small room, while the senator was given the keys to a magnificent mansion.

The cardinal asked, "Why do I get a tiny one-room place and the senator gets very special treatment?"

Saint Peter said, "Well, we've got lots of professional

clergy up here, but he's the very first Senator we have ever seen!"

⁓

When Fred arrived at the Pearly Gates, he was met by an official angelic being who began to process his entry data. Fred was asked for some purely unselfish, kindly deed he had done on earth.

Fred thought about it and said, "Oh yes. I have something that might interest you. One day I came upon a little old lady who was being beaten by a motorcycle gang member who was stealing her purse. I just stepped right up and kicked over his motorcycle just to distract him. Then I kicked him real hard in the shins and shouted at her to run for help. And I hauled off and gave the guy a hard right to the chin."

The angel looked at Fred with a great deal of interest and said, "That's quite a story. I'm impressed." Then taking his clipboard in hand, he said, "Could you tell me just when this happened?"

Fred looked at his watch and said, "Oh, about two or three minutes ago!"

⁓

The pastor was speaking about heaven, about eternal bliss and the joys that are waiting for every person on the other side. He paused for effect and asked, "How many of you here want to go to heaven?"

All hands went up except for an elderly man sitting in the front pew. The minister asked, "Sir, don't you want to go to heaven along with the rest of us?"

The man replied, "Yes, but I thought you were making up a load to go right now!"

⌒

"Aim at heaven and you will get earth thrown in. Aim at earth, you will get neither." —C. S. Lewis

⌒

Another Man's Wife?

This allegedly took place in a downtown, first-church, high-steeple, formal, historic kind of a church attended by only a few members. The frustrated associate pastor approached the much more experienced senior pastor and told him that he was ready to give up, resign, move on to someplace else, or do another kind of a job. The veteran pastor patiently inquired as to the reason.

The young assistant said, "Whenever I lead worship or make announcements, as you have hired me to do, nobody pays attention. They talk to each other; they read bulletins; they read hand-out papers—anything but give me their attention!"

The senior pastor, after thinking a minute, replied: "You're doing it all wrong; it's really simple. Now, let's think about this. First, it's important that you stride with vigor to the pulpit, act as if you're completely in charge, and this will help to get you noticed. Then you need to dramatically say something that really gets their undivided attention."

The associate nodded and responded, "Okay, that gives me some help. I'll practice until I get it down."

Then the senior pastor added, "In a few weeks we'll be celebrating Mother's Day. Next Sunday, why not start off the announcements by saying something like this: 'Some of the most wonderful moments of my life have been spent in the arms of another man's wife.' Now that will get their attention!

You should then pause for effect as they will be really looking at you. Then tell them, 'This other man's wife was my mother.' Then I'll step to the pulpit with the announcement about our upcoming activities and plans for a special Mother's Day service. Got it? This will be dramatic and attention-getting."

So the next Sunday rolled around, and the associate had been practicing this special attention-getting announcement. In fact, he was quite pleased with his progress. Exactly at the starting time of 10:30 a.m., he strode to the pulpit with purpose and vigor, and in his loudest voice, announced: "Some of the most wonderful moments of my life have been spent in the arms of another man's wife!" He paused for dramatic effect and looked out at the crowd.

He had their attention. Ushers stopped moving; people slid to the front of their pews; all talking ceased; bulletins were put down; mothers placed their hands over the ears of innocent children. The silence was pregnant with expectation. Time stood still; people looked at each other; some were shocked; deacons were looking for other deacons; some reached for their cell phones; it was dramatic, even historic! And how he was enjoying the moment! It was working to perfection! This was a very different beginning to a typical Sunday morning experience!

However, what he hadn't done was to tell his little red-headed wife about this new and dramatic approach! She exploded and slammed down her hymnbook, threw her purse on the seat with a thump, crumpled and flung her bulletin with a flourish of white-hot anger, and started for him by climbing out of the pew.

Hurriedly, flustered, losing his train of thought, he stammered, "For the life of me, I can't remember who she was!"

So the ransomed of the Lord shall return, and come to Zion with singing, with everlasting joy on their heads. They shall obtain joy and gladness; sorrow and sighing shall flee away (Isaiah 51:11).

BUT SERIOUSLY FOLKS: Preachers have been and are some of the most hilarious people on earth. Sometimes it's the only thing that helps them keep their sanity. When a preacher pulls a blooper or guffaw, no one in the congregation ever lets it be forgotten! Better to forgive and forget.

LET THE CATS OUT...
Something you can learn about life from your cat: Life is hard, then you nap.

God Rest Ye Merry Clergy Persons

A certain church found itself burdened with a very tedious, stuffy, boring, and self-centered pastor for a couple of years. Finally the day came when he was called to another church. He announced his resignation by saying: "Brethren and sisters, the same Lord who sent me to you is now calling me away." There was a moment of silence and quickly the congregation rose as one and began to sing: "What a Friend We Have in Jesus!"

A preacher and his congregation had strained relations, and after more than a few squabbles and battles he was appointed as chaplain at the state prison. Elated to be finally rid of him so easily, the people came and packed the church to hear his farewell sermon. He chose for his text: "I go and prepare a place for you...that where I am, there you may be also" (John 14:3).

Three boys, at recess, were bragging about their dads. The first said: "My dad scribbles a few words on a piece of paper, he calls it a poem, and they give him $250."

The second said, "That's nothing. My dad scribbles a few words on a piece of paper, he calls it a song, and they give him $500!"

The third said, "I got you both beat. My dad scribbles a few words on a piece of paper, he calls it a sermon, and it takes eight people to collect all the money!"

After the birth of their child, an Episcopal priest, wearing his clerical collar, visited his wife in the hospital. He greeted her with a long hug and a mushy kiss. Then he gave her another hug and another kiss as he left.

Later, the wife's hospital roommate commented, "Your pastor is sure a whole lot more friendlier than mine."

It happened in a rural church in southwestern Kansas. The pastor announced, "I have been asked by the elders to pray for rain because of the drought." Then he paused and looked down at the group of elders seated in the front pew and said, "I am not going to do it. You knew for a week I was going to pray for rain, but none of you brought an umbrella!"

A seminary president told the following story: When candidates are ordained into the ministry, they have one thing to do in the service. At the conclusion of worship, the candidate stands, walks up the steps into the chancel, turns, and gives the benediction. That is their first act as an ordained pastor.

One candidate stood, approached the steps, and ascended. But on the first step, he stepped inside the hem of his robe. Now the obvious thing to do would be to step back out of the robe, but he didn't—he kept on up the steps, all the time walking up the inside of his robe. Finally, at the top of the steps, looking like a dwarf in a white tent, he turned around. His robe could not turn with him since he was standing inside it. Turning he placed the left arm of his robe right in the center of his chest and the right arm between his shoulders. All he could move was his wrist, with which he waved as he gave the benediction. When he was done, two ushers came forward, picked him up by the arms, and carried him off like a piece of furniture. I wish I could have been there to see it! —*Rev. William Goodin*

The pulpit in a church in Idaho was one of those raised affairs, and I was the visiting guest speaker. Once you climbed the five or six steps up to the pulpit, you closed the door behind you. Now, I have always preached from the back of the pulpit area. About three-quarters of the way through my sermon, I made a dramatic point, accidentally knocked the door open behind me, and fell backward out of the pulpit. The organist immediately started playing, the offering was taken, and I managed to limp out to the altar to receive it and conclude the service. After the service was over, no one said a thing. Finally one elderly gentleman said to me: "Pastor, I'll say one thing for you, when you get done preaching, you really quit!" —*Rev. William Goodin*

Pastor Steve Warriner of Abundant Life Assembly was teaching on the garments of the Old Testament high priest. There are many gemstones of truth in this area of the Bible. However, the Sunday morning crowd roared with laughter as the pastor spoke of the bells and pomegranates that lined the bottom of the priestly garment. He explained it like this: "Every time he took a step, he tinkled!"

The picture of modern combines moving through a wheat field and harvesting the grain makes for great imagery. While preaching about the field being "white unto harvest," the pastor said: "The farmer prepares diligently. Then he goes out and gets in his concubine and rides into the field for harvest."

Laughter in the House

Pastor Chesser was preaching. "We can enjoy the journey to heaven. Our walk on this earth ought to be exciting. Like John the Baptist, we can be joyful along this journey." Chesser suddenly remembered that John had his head cut off after only six months of ministry. Then he momentarily forgot other important facts about John. But then, his mind began to regain clarity and he said: "Like John the Baptist, we need to take a barrel of locusts and two wild honeys and head for the wilderness!"

Heard over the loudspeakers in the hallway of this church: "Please, dear friends, it's time to start the service. Don't just stand in the lobby scratching your head...come into the auditorium and pick your seat!"

Following a wedding, an unnamed pastor announced that the "conception" would take place in the church's social hall.

Children don't always hear correctly. A little boy wanted to know why the pastor always prayed in the "name of the Father, Son, and Whole East Coast!"

The visiting evangelist had preached a powerful sermon against drinking, especially whiskey, and concluded the message by saying, "Every drop of the nasty stuff should be poured in the river!"

The worship leader stood and led in the closing hymn: "Shall We Gather at the River!"

After the church service, while greeting parishioners at the door, a pastor told a woman: "I noticed your husband walked out in the middle of my sermon. I hope I didn't say something that offended him."

"Not at all," she replied. "My husband has been walking in his sleep for years."

A member of his congregation told Reverend Keating the best prayer he had ever heard was this one by a church elder: "Dear God, please help me be the person my dog thinks I am."

After a Sunday morning service, a small boy told the family's pastor: "When I grow up, I'm going to give you some money."

"Well, thank you," the pastor replied, "but why?"

"Because my daddy says you're one of the poorest preachers we've ever had."

You Just Can't Have Church Without One of Those Hand-Out Papers...

(It's Time for Bulletin Bloopers!)

No respectable book on clean humor is complete without a section on church bulletins. Remember, a good church bulletin has something for everyone, even for those who look for the typos and unintential bloopers. So here are some that were found in bulletins across the country:

• There will be no healing service this Sunday due to the pastor's illness.

• Not everyone who attends this church has been converted...so please watch your handbags and wallets.

• Sermon Title: "How Much Should a Christian Drink?" This sermon will be followed by a full choir.

• There will be a mating of the singles in the basement following this service. All young men and woman should be there.

• Don't forget that the mobile X-ray unit will be here in the church parking lot on Tuesday. It will examine you for tuberculosis and other diseases which you'll receive free of charge.

- This being Easter Sunday, we will ask Mrs. Stanley to come forward and lay an egg on the altar.

- This afternoon there will be a meeting in the south and north ends of the church. Children will be baptized at both ends.

- Tuesday, at 4:00 p.m., there will be an ice cream social. All ladies giving milk, come early.

- The service will close with "Little Drops of Water." One of the ladies will start quietly and the rest of the congregation will join.

- Next Sunday, a special collection will be taken to defray the expense of the new carpet. All those wishing to do something on the new carpet, come forward and get a piece of paper.

- The ladies of the church have cast off clothing of every kind and they may be seen in the basement on this Friday afternoon.

- A bean supper will be held Saturday evening in the church basement. Music will follow.

- The rosebud on the altar this morning is to announce the birth of David Alan Anderson, the sin of Reverend and Mrs. Anderson.

- For those of you who have children and don't know it, we have a nursery downstairs.

- Clothes are being collected for the Guatemala Orphanage. Ladies who can drive by the church office and drop off their clothes will be given prompt attention.

- The pastor will preach his farewell sermon, after which the choir will sing: "Break Forth into Joy!"

- Pray for those sick of the church.

- Let's hold the Bored of the church up in prayer.

- The music for today's service was all composed by George Frederick Handel in celebration of the 300th anniversary of his birth.

- Don't let worry kill you off...let the church help.

- A songfest will be hell at the Methodist Church this Wednesday.

- The ice cream social at the church parsonage was a success. Singing was enjoyed by all. The pastor's wife labored all evening at the piano which, as usual, fell upon her.

- The singles will present Shakespeare's *Hamlet* at their dinner theater in the church basement on Saturday evening at 7:00 p.m. The whole church is invited to attend this tragedy.

- Ninety-four-year-old Hazel had died and the bulletin noted her written wish: "There will be no male pallbearers. They wouldn't take me out when I was alive; I don't want them to take me out when I'm dead!"

Humor and the Presidency

Humor is where you find it, and what better place than the White House? Donald Rumsfeld, the former Secretary of Defense who returned for another stint in the Bush II administration, made some interesting comments on the subject of humor and the presidency:

"There are all kinds of humor that a president can use. Jack Kennedy, of course, was a great wit. As president, he used what you might call 'deflecting' humor. For example, I recall there was a big to-do over the fact that Stewart Udall, his interior secretary, had been extracting campaign contributions from all the major corporations that were beholden to the interior department. As a result, the press was just all over him.

Things reached a fever pitch the night of a major black-tie fund-raising dinner. But Kennedy was wonderful. He got up and thanked the guests for their wonderful generosity, he thanked the chairmen of all committees for their hard work, and he thanked Stewart Udall for handling the publicity. At that moment, the problem was gone. It was over." I'd say it was dissolved in the sea of laughter.

Then, there's also what could be called "gallows" humor. President Gerald Ford remembered how upset Senator Bob Mathias was at the Republican convention. Mathias, of course, was a liberal Republican and he was bordering on apoplectic over the party's nomination of ultra conservative Barry Goldwater. This particular night he was standing in the back of the hall, while down in front, Dwight Eisenhower was giving a speech. And he heard Mathias mumble, as he thought about Goldwater becoming the Republican candidate, "This would never have happened if Eisenhower was still alive."

⌒

Businessmen who come to Washington bring what you might call "industrial" humor, according to former President Gerald Ford. "I recently took part in a panel discussion with a number of former White House chiefs-of-staff at which General Andrew Goodpaster, who worked for President Eisenhower, provided an excellent example of industrial humor. During the Eisenhower administration, this super efficient Pentagon briefer addressed a special meeting of the National Security Council. He had flip charts and he had visual aids. He was supposed to be on for twelve minutes, and he was on for exactly twelve minutes. He had a three-part presentation, each part of which had three parts. He took three questions and then he walked out.

"When the guy was gone, Charlie Wilson, the former head of General Motors who was Eisenhower's secretary of defense, turned to Goodpaster and said, 'You know, that fella's got too much horsepower for his flywheel!'"

⌒

Here's another by President Ford:

"There are two ways to become an authority on humor," noted Ford. "The first way is to be one of the perpetrators. You know them: comedians, satirists, cartoonists, and impersonators. The second way is to be the victim of their merciless talents. As such a victim, I take a backseat to no one as far as humor is concerned."

Ford was one of the best-natured and best-liked presidents, and he was also the butt of more than his share of jokes—not all of them kind, either. He talks about what it's like to take a header down the steps of Air Force One and then have everyone make jokes about it like, "As I was picking myself up, Dave Kennerly said, 'Nice of you to drop in!'"

Edward Bennett Williams notes, "Humor is indispensable to democracy."

You have loved righteousness and hated lawlessness; therefore God, Your God, has anointed You with the oil of gladness more than Your companions (Hebrews 1:9).

BUT SERIOUSLY FOLKS: "Unlike freedom of speech or freedom of the press," the former President Ford pointed out, "laughter is not specifically protected by an amendment to our Constitution. Nevertheless, it is probably the clearest and most resounding expression of freedom we have." Then he also added, "You might as well laugh at yourself because you can be sure others are going to laugh at you."

LET THE CATS OUT...
If you put off making the bed in the morning until the cat gets up—you might be a cat lover.

Politicians and Their Parties

During a heated debate in the U.S. Senate, one senator told another to "go to Hades!" The senator under attack appealed to the presiding Vice President Calvin Coolidge concerning the propriety of the remark.

Coolidge, who had been idly leafing through a book, looked up and said, "I've been going through the rule book. You don't have to go."
—*John L. May of St. Louis, Missouri*

A Sunday school teacher asked her class: "Who decreed that all the world should be taxed?"

"The Democrats!" shouted a little girl.

Israeli Prime Minister Yitzhak Shamir and President George Bush scheduled a meeting. When Shamir arrived late, Bush let him know he did not like to be kept waiting.

Shamir replied, "I'm sorry, Mr. President. I was meeting with someone more important than you are."

"Who is more important than the president of the United States?" Bush asked.

Shamir replied: "I was meeting with Moses."

"You know Moses?" Bush exclaimed. "Get him on the phone. I want to talk to him."

Shamir picked up the phone, dialed, listened, and then hung up. "He doesn't want to talk to you," he told Bush. "He said the last time he talked to a bush it cost him forty years in the wilderness!"

—*Evelyn Brisco of Okmulgee, Oklahoma*

In Washington, D.C., a visitor asked a security guard on C Street, "Which side is the State Department on?"

The reply, "Ours, I hope."

If you think you're getting too much government, just be thankful you're not getting as much as you're paying for.

When Edward Everett Hale was chaplain of the U.S.

Senate, he was asked, "Do you pray for the senators, Dr. Hale?"

He replied, "No, I look at the senators and pray for the country."

A surgeon, an engineer, and a politician were debating which of their professions was the oldest. The surgeon said, "Eve was made from Adam's rib, and that, of course, was a surgical procedure. Obviously, surgery is the oldest profession."

The engineer countered, "Yes, but before that, order was created out of chaos, and that most certainly was an engineering job."

The politician smiled and said triumphantly, "Aha! And just who do you think created the chaos?"

A freshman politician was in Washington, D.C. for his orientation. He also visited in the home of the ranking senator who was attempting to interpret the bizarre wonder of the Capitol. As they stood looking over the Potomac River, an old, rotten deteriorating log floated by on the river. The old-timer said: "This city is much like that log out there."

The fledgling politician asked: "How is that?"

The senator replied, "Well, there are probably about 100,000 grubs, ants, worms, bugs, and critters on that old log as it floats down the river. And I imagine every one of them thinks that it is steering it."

When a prominent office holder in Washington died, a perennial office seeker hurried to the White House to tell the president that he'd like to "take the deceased man's place."

The president replied, "If it's all right with the undertaker, it's all right with me."

—

"And now, ladies and gentlemen," continued the congressman, "I want to tax your memories!"

"Good gracious," muttered one colleague to another. "Why haven't we thought of that before?"

Some of the World's Worst...

OPENING CEREMONIES: Wishing to open their new pistol range in style, the officials of Brigham City decided to invite a team of crack marksmen from the Utah Police Force. The idea was that one of them would step forward and break the ceremonial ribbon with a single bullet.

Five hundred bullets later, the ribbon remained impressively unspoiled and untouched! According to an eyewitness, it was only cut when one officer stepped forward and "let go with a shotgun blast" at point-blank range, finally leaving the ribbon in smoldering shreds!

MILITARY TOP SECRETS: The *F-19 Stealth Fighter* plane was so secret that not even American senators voting for its billion-dollar cost were allowed to see the plans or a rendering of the finished product. It was so secret that the Pentagon refused to even acknowledge the existence of the so-called invisible fighter!

In July of 1986 "Testor Toys" produced a model kit for the F-19 and more than 100,000 kids bought them in toy and model stores for $9.95 each, giving their senators a first look before they rolled off the assembly line. When these facts were pointed out to the manufacturers, they replied, "You've got to have a bit of mystery about it. That makes it exciting!"

BATON TWIRLING: Noted for the height, range, and drama of their twirls, members of the Ventura Baton Twirling Troupe surprised even themselves on this one occasion. During that year's Independence Day march, one of the batons hit a power cable, blacked out the area, started a grass fire, and put the local radio station off the air. "They were on form," the mayor commented, trying to spin it positively.

"Therefore do not worry about tomorrow, for tomorrow will worry about its own things. Sufficient for the day is its own trouble" (Matthew 6:34).

BUT SERIOUSLY FOLKS: Humans can easily be overrated, but mankind's real genius lies in quite the opposite direction. Being really bad at something requires skill, panache, and blatant individualism. People who are bad at their chosen endeavors have names that will shine as beacons for future generations. It seems as though homo sapiens will continue to have more inglorious feats. Such actions illustrate that there really are no limits to what humanity can achieve, but they sure make for a good laugh!

LET THE CATS OUT...
"There are two means of refuge from the miseries of life: music and cats." —*Albert Schweitzer*

Happiness and Joy

Baptist pastor Carl Winters is one cleric who appreciates the value of being joyful and happy. Mostly he appreciates the value of laughter.

He says, "When I preach, I definitely try to make people laugh. And while their mouths are open, I put something in for them to chew on."

The late Pope John XXIII granted a private audience to a newly appointed cardinal who complained that the responsibilities of his new office were robbing him of his joy and causing him to lose sleep.

Pope John replied, "The very same thing happened to me in the first weeks of my pontificate." He continued reassuring him, "But then one day my guardian angel appeared to me in a daydream and whispered, 'Giovanni, don't take yourself so seriously.' And ever since then I have been happy and able to sleep!"

A preacher felt badly because he had just been defeated soundly on the golf course by one of his parishioners, a man thirty years his senior. "Cheer up, Reverend," said his older opponent. "You'll have the joy in the end. You'll be burying me someday."

"Even then," replied the preacher, "it will be your hole."

A senior citizen had just completed his annual physical exam and was waiting for the doctor's report. After a few minutes, the doctor came in with his charts in his hand and said: "There's no reason why you can't live a completely normal life as long as you don't try to enjoy it."

Question: "Why did the Israelites wander forty years in the desert wilderness?"

Answer: "Even back then the men would not stop and ask for directions!"

My wife and I were at the beach when I said, "You know, I'm fifty-six. I'm middle-aged."

She said, "How many men do you know over 112?"

Quotable Quotes

It's so important to know you can choose to feel good. Most people don't think they have that choice.
—*Neil Simon*

Jewish spirituality has always found a place for joy and humor. It has not forgotten that the biblical God is a God of unexpected turns, twists, and surprises. God plays; God teases! Jewish spirituality loves gaining humorous insights from religion. Even the classics...the Talmud, the Zohar, the Hasidic stories...revel in the joyful tidbit: "If one man calls you an ass, ignore it. If two or three call you an ass, start looking for a saddle!"
—*Matthias Newman*

Joy and happiness and a knowledge of the Bible will improve your face value!
—*George Goldtrap*

Beware of the man whose belly does not move when he laughs.
—*Old Chinese Proverb*

Happiness always sneaks in through a door you didn't know was open.
—*John Barrymore*

Money can't buy happiness. It just helps you look for it in more places. When happiness shows up, please give it a comfortable seat.

Fractured Parables...

A man from the back country up in the hills, wished to begin a second career by entering the ministry. He applied to a denominational credentialing committee. The day of his personal interview arrived, and to the best of my ability, the following conversation has been reconstructed to resemble the interview that supposedly took place:

"Which part of the Bible do you prefer, Sam?" came the first question.

"The book of the parables," was his reply.

"Just which book are you referring to?"

"The book of Mark."

"And which one of the parables is your choice?" asked a committee member.

"Well, gentlemen, the parable of the Good Samaritan is my specialty."

"Okay, then Sam, please, will you tell us the parable of the Good Samaritan?"

"Yes, sirs, I will. Once there was this man travelin' from Jerusalem to Jericho and he fell among thorns, an' the thorns sprang up an' choked him. An' as he went on, he didn't have no money an' he met the Queen of Sheba, an' she gave him one thousand talents of gold an' one hundred changes of raiment. An' he got into a chariot an' drove furiously, an' when he was drivin' under a big juniper tree, his hair caught on the limb of the tree an' he hung there many days, an' the ravens brought him food to eat an' water to drink an' he ate five thousand loaves of bread an' two fishes! One night when he was hangin' there asleep, his wife, Delilah, came along an' cut off his hair, an' he dropped, an' he fell on stony ground. But he got up an' went on, an' it began to rain, an' it rained forty days an' forty nights, an' he hid hisself in a cave, an' he lived on locusts an' wild honey." He paused to catch his breath, looked at the committee members, and continued...

"Then he went on 'til he met a servant who said, 'Come, take supper at my house!' An' he made an excuse an' said, "No, I won't. I have married a wife an' I can't go!' An' the servant went out in the highways an' in the hedges and compelled him to come in. After supper he went on an' came on down to Jericho. An' when he got there he looked up an' saw that ol' Queen Jezebel sitting down away up high in a window. An' she laughed at him, an' he said, 'Throw her down out of there!' An' they throwed her down. An' he said, 'Throw her down again!' An' they throwed her down seventy times seven, and of the fragments that remained, they picked up twelve baskets full, besides women and children, an' they say, 'Blessed are the piece-makers.' Now...whose wife do you think she will be in the Judgment Day?"

◆

Okay, what more can be said? Not much...other than the fact is that some of God's choicest servants have been joyful people with a highly developed sense of humor. For example, consider Oswald Chambers, the man who wrote what can be considered the most widely read devotional book of all time, *My Utmost for His Highest!* He was also known for his rollicking sense of humor. After meeting Chambers for the first time, one very serious young preacher said, "I was shocked at what I then considered his undue levity. He was the most irreverent Reverend I had ever met!"

On another occasion, Chambers was speaking with a disillusioned young soldier, who said to him, "I hate religious people."

To which Chambers replied, "So do I." And with that issue settled, he listened to this young man's heartbreaking story and gently directed him into a meaningful relationship with Jesus Christ.

Be diligent to present yourself approved to God, a worker who does not need to be ashamed, rightly dividing the word of truth (2 Timothy 2:15).

BUT SERIOUSLY FOLKS: Just because you have disciplined yourself to live a joyful and joy-filled life doesn't mean you can't be serious when the time calls for it. A well-developed sense of humor is described as being "life's bumper!"

LET THE CATS OUT...
Dogs come when you call; cats have an answering machine and will think about getting back to you.

A Church Can Be a Very Funny Place

This is a copy of a prayer posted by a particular church in the meeting room that housed the weekly gathering of seniors:

Lord, Thou knowest better than I know myself that I am growing older.

Keep me from getting too talkative, and thinking I must say something on every subject and on every occasion.

Release me from craving to straighten out everybody's affairs.

Teach me the glorious lesson that occasionally it is possible that I may be mistaken.

Make me thoughtful, but not moody; helpful, but not bossy.

Thou knowest, Lord, that what I want most is a few friends at the end!

—Bennett Cerf

Things weren't going too well in the first-grade Sunday school class. Nobody seemed able to recall from a lesson the identity of Saint Matthew, nor did they do any better with

Saint Mark. Finally, the teacher hopefully asked, "Surely somebody will remember who Peter was?"

A small boy in the last row came to the rescue. "Teacher," he piped up, "wasn't he a wabbit?"

E. H. Taylor tells this tale at the expense of Bishop Bompas, the first Anglican missionary to venture into the Yukon territories.

The good bishop discovered a tribe of Indians who had never recorded a baptism, a confirmation, or even a marriage ceremony. He set about changing this situation by baptizing and confirming, and hastily wound it up by willy-nilly uniting couples in holy wedlock.

Later the tribal chief told Bishop Bompas that his tribe hadn't had so much fun in a month of Sundays. "What part of the ceremonies," asked the bishop, "did you enjoy the most?"

"The marriage service," replied the chief, happily. "We all got new wives!"

An usher is passing a collection plate at a church wedding. He is explaining to each row as he offers the plate, "I admit, it's a bit extraordinary, but the bride's father insisted on it."

An inactive church member had become critically ill with a heart attack. At that same moment in time he also inherited $100,000 from a deceased relative. But his wife, thinking the shock of the good news might be a tipping point and cause so much excitement he might die, asked the pastor to break the news gently to him.

"Brother Jones," the pastor gently explained, "I know you have never tithed or given much to our church, but God has been very good to you anyway. He has given you a $100,000 inheritance because your relative has just died."

"Great!" replied the sick man. "That means when I get well and get to church, I can give a $10,000 tithe check to the church in a couple of Sundays!"

You guessed it! The pastor had a heart attack!

Anybody who thinks our government is concerned about there being a shortage of coins in circulation hasn't been to a church lately.

When it comes to giving...some people stop at nothing!

A strong missionary appeal had just been made, and the offering plate was now being passed. The little old lady began fumbling in her purse. The nearer the ushers came, the more frantically she searched her bag. Finally, noticing her plight, a small boy sitting nearby slid over and nudged her. "Here, lady," he said. "You take my dime. I can hide under the seat."

A pastor and wife were driving to visit Grandma and Grandpa for the holidays. Their daughter Rachel asked the inevitable question: "Are we almost there?"

The father said, "No, we are still 150 miles away."

She asked, "Well, how long is that?"

"Well, Rachel, it's about three more hours."

She didn't say anything for a few moments as she thought about how long three hours would be. Then she leaned forward from the backseat, making sure she could see her mother's face, and asked, "Mommy, is that as long as one of Daddy's sermons?"

Imagine yourself going down the road of life and you come to a vital crossroads. Standing at this junction are the following three figures: a pastor who never finishes his sermon until late Saturday night; a pastor who always has his sermon finished and polished by Thursday noon, and the Easter Bunny. Which of these three would you ask for directions?

The answer is: the pastor who never finishes his sermon until late Saturday night because the other two are figments of your imagination!

~

The easiest way to stay awake during a sermon is to deliver it! I never heard a sermon without getting some good out of it. However, I've had some mighty close calls.

~

During a communion service in our church in Parsons, Kansas, my wife, Betty, was sitting in the third row with Caroline Divine, the wife of one of our deacons. Philip, our eight-year-old, and David, Carolyn's seven-year-old, were in the row in front of them. When the communion trays were served in their row, Philip and David helped themselves. When I said, "Let us all drink together," the two horrified mothers watched as Philip and David clicked their communion cups together, exclaimed, "Cheers!" turned up their cups, and drank it all!

—*Pastor Warren McPherson*

~

During an ecumenical gathering, a passerby burst into the meeting shouting, "THE CHURCH IS ON FIRE!"

The Baptists shouted, "Quick, everybody into the baptismal tank!"

The Methodists gathered into a corner and prayed!

The Congregationalists hollered, "Everybody for himself or herself!"

The Seventh-Day Adventists proclaimed, "The world is coming to an end because it's the vengeance of an angry God!"

The Lutherans posted a thesis notice with 96 points declaring that the fire was evil because it was the abode of the devil!

The Christian Scientists agreed among themselves that there really was not a fire!

The Presbyterians appointed a chairperson who was to appoint a committee to look into the matter of the fire and report at the next meeting.

The Episcopalians formed an orderly procession and marched out together!

The Unitarian-Universalists concluded that the fire had as much right to be there as anyone else did!

The Mormons quickly began to gather food and clothing and other essentials for the survivors of the fire!

The Catholics passed the collection plates to cover the costs of the damages!

The Charismatic-Pentecostals began shouting and praising the Lord because revival had come and the fire of the Holy Spirit was falling!

The Salvation Army struck up the band and played "When the Saints Go Marching Out!"

The Calvinists said, "This is God's will!"

And...a little boy pulled out his cell phone and dialed 911 for help!

In Sunday school, a teacher asked her class why they thought the clergyman in the Good Samaritan story walked by on the other side of the road. "Because the man lying by the roadside had already been robbed," a little girl responded!

The Short Diary of a Floridian and His Wife
Who Moved to Minnesota to Retire

NOVEMBER 23: It's starting to snow! The really first one of the season, which I understand, is a bit later than usual and the first snow we have seen in many, many years. The wife and I took our hot chocolate and sat by the picture window, watching the soft, large, beautiful flakes slowly drift down. They clung to bare tree branches and gently covered the ground. It was gorgeous—a winter wonderland!

DECEMBER 1: This morning we awoke to a lovely blanket of crystal white snow covering the landscape. What a fantastic sight! Every tree and shrub covered with a beautiful white mantle. I shoveled snow for the first time and loved it. It was great exercise—so invigorating! I did both our driveway and sidewalk. I waved at the neighbors. Later that day, a city snowplow came along and accidentally covered our driveway with compacted snow from the street. The operator smiled and waved. I waved back and shoveled it clear again.

DECEMBER 9: It snowed an additional eight inches last night and the temperature dropped to two degrees below zero! Invigorating! Several limbs on the trees and shrubs snapped due to the weight of the snow. I shoveled our driveway again. The snowplow dumped a brownish-grayish, compacted snow from the street on my drive. Shoveled again.

DECEMBER 10: Warmed up enough during the day to create some slush, which soon became ice when the temperature dropped again. Bought snow tires for both cars. Fell on my behind in the driveway. Only $175 to a chiropractor, but nothing is broken. More ice and snow expected. Shoveled snow.

DECEMBER 11: Snowed again, not quite enough to shovel, but on top of the ice it is really slick. Below zero! Sold the wife's car and bought a 4X4 SUV in order to get her to work. Slid into a guardrail anyway and did considerable damage to the right rear quarter panel on the new 4X4. Had another ten inches of the white crud last night. Both vehicles are now covered in salt and crud. More shoveling for me today. That stinking snowplow came by twice today; the crud is brownish-grayish and freezes as soon as it hits my driveway. Had to shovel out three times!

DECEMBER 12: Twenty degrees below zero this morning and a wind chill on top of it. More cruddy white stuff. Not a tree or shrub on our property that hasn't been damaged! Power off most of the night. Tried to keep from freezing to death with candles, fireplace, and a kerosene heater, which tipped over and nearly burned our house down. I managed to put out the flames but suffered second-degree burns on my hands and lost all my eyelashes and eyebrows. Car slid on ice on way to emergency room. Lost control and it was totaled.

DECEMBER 14: More stinking white crud keeps on coming down. Have to put on all the clothes we own just to get to the stupid mailbox. If I ever catch that jerk who operates the snowplow, I'll tell him a thing or two. I think he hides around the corner and waits for me to finish shoveling and then comes roaring down the street about 100 miles per hour, flinging snow everywhere and buries our driveway and

mailbox again! Power went off again today. Toilet froze up
and broke and part of the roof leaks water and has begun to
cave in. More shoveling!

DECEMBER 16: Eighteen more inches of stinking
snow-crud along with nasty sleet covers everything, including
the streets. Only heaven knows how much is falling today. I
went after the snowplow jerk with a shovel but he managed
to get away. Wife flew back to Florida. Car won't
start...second 4X4 won't start! Gave up shoveling!

DECEMBER 18: A white Christmas is almost here. Do
I care? Thirty-five degrees below zero and a wind chill so
cold it can't be measured! I'm going snow blind. My toe, ears,
and my hands are all frostbitten. Emergency room this time.
Haven't seen the sun in weeks. More snow predicted tomorrow. I'm taking the next flight out, putting the house up
for sale, and moving back south no matter what!

*Have you entered the treasury of snow, or have you seen
the treasury of hail, which I have reserved for the time of
trouble, for the day of battle and war?* (Job 38:22–23).

BUT SERIOUSLY FOLKS: There may be a few things in
life that cannot be improved by a good laugh, but not many.
You're probably too old to cry, and nobody really wants to cry
with you anyway. But you can smile and find that the smile is
contagious and others will smile with you. In regards to the
weather, we don't really know what it will be tomorrow, but we
do know that it will eventually change!

LET THE CATS OUT...
Something you can learn about life from your cat: Nap often.

A Blooper Is a Stupid Mistake, or It Can Be a Fly That Falls Just Beyond the Infield for a Hit

A little girl walked into a small town grocery store, placed an earthen jar on the counter, and asked for two dollars' worth of honey. Soon the jar was filled. She picked up the jar and started for the door. The storekeeper stopped her and asked if she had forgotten to pay for her mother's honey.

"No sir, I thought you got the money," the startled youngster replied. "My mother put it into the jar for you."

Scott Widmer, Methodist pastor, reported the following foot/mouth incident: It was more embarrassing than hilarious at the time. "I was using John Wesley's Covenant Renewal Service on New Year's Eve, one line of which goes: 'Let us bind ourselves with willing bonds to our covenant God.' The way it came out was: 'Let us bind ourselves with willing blondes...'"

The annual children's Christmas program got off to a great start. The place was filled with parents and grandparents, aunts and uncles, and friends. When the curtain was raised, there was a momentary silence followed by a roar of laughter. One of the teachers rushed up on stage to reposition the four first-grade girls who stood behind the manger scene. They each held a placard and together they were to spell out S-T-A-R. The girls in their excitement had lined up backward and proudly held their signs aloft and spelled: R-A-T-S!

In November of 1980, Texaco oil field workers in Louisiana erected the latest in oil drilling rigs at Lake Peigneur.

After only a few hours of drilling they sat back, expecting oil to shoot up. Instead, however, they watched a whirlpool form, sucking down not only the entire 1,300-acre lake, but also five houses, nine barges, eight tugboats, two oil-drilling rigs, a mobile home, most of a botanical garden, and 10 percent of nearby Jefferson Island, leaving a half-mile wide crater!

No one had told them that there was an abandoned salt mine under the lake! A local fisherman said he thought the world was coming to an end.

One of the greatest linemen to ever play football was the All-Pro defensive specialist Jim Marshall of the Minnesota Vikings. On October 26, 1964, in a game against the San Francisco 49ers, he managed to crown his glorious career by grabbing a 49er fumble, sprinting sixty yards the wrong way down Kezar Stadium, and scoring a touchdown for the opposition.

This sort of touchdown is harder to achieve because, first, you have to beat the defensive attempts of the opposing side and then he had to beat his own team too! He had the entire

Minnesota team along with those on their bench chasing him down the sideline, yelling and waving their arms, attempting to tackle him, but he was focused on the goal. Later Marshall said he thought they were just celebrating with him!

After the game, with a modesty common to all great athletes, he said: "I just picked up the ball and started running!"

One of the most exciting archaeological finds of the century was made by a team of researchers in Tehran who uncovered the skeleton of a dinosaur that had only previously been found in North America.

The ribs and vertebrae were carefully preserved, and in 1930, a scientific mission from Madrid flew out to conduct a thorough examination.

Things got even more exciting when their final report announced that the reptile was, in fact, an abandoned ancient hay-making machine that had been caught in a landslide!

Until recently the world record for flunking a driver's test was held by Mrs. Helen Ireland of Auburn, California, who failed it in the first seconds. She cleverly mistook the accelerator for the brake and shot straight through the wall of the test center!

This seemed unbeatable until 1991, when a Lanarkshire mechanic named Thomson failed the test before the examiner had even gotten into the car. Arriving at the test center, he tooted the horn to summon the examiner, who strode out to the vehicle, said it was illegal to sound your horn while stationary, announced that Thomson had failed the test, wrote him out a citation, and strode back in again.

Genius of this kind cannot be taught. It must be a natural gift!

The Safety Bulletin

To The Worker's Compensation Court:

I am writing this in response to your letter regarding my Worker's Compensation injury report form.

In block #3 of the accident report form, I put "poor planning" as the cause of my accident. You said in your letter that I should explain more fully, and I trust the following will be sufficient.

I am a bricklayer by trade. On the day of the accident, I was working alone on the roof of a new six-story building. When I completed my work, I discovered that I had about 500 pounds of brick left over. Rather than carry the bricks down by hand, I decided to lower them in a barrel by using a pulley and rope, which was still attached to the side of the building at the sixth floor. This had been used in the construction.

Securing the rope at ground level, I went back up to the roof, swung the barrel out, and loaded the brick into it. Then I went back down to the ground level and untied the rope, then holding it tightly to insure a slow descent of the 500 pounds of brick.

You will note in block #11 that I weigh 145 pounds.

Due to my surprise at being jerked off the ground so suddenly, I lost my presence of mind and forgot to let go of the rope. Needless to say, I proceeded at a rather rapid rate of speed up the side of the building.

In the vicinity of the third floor, I met the barrel coming down. This explains the fractured nose and lacerated skull and broken collarbone.

Slowed only slightly, I continued my rapid ascent, not stopping until the fingers of my right hand were squashed down deep into the pulley. This accounts for the broken fingers on my right hand.

At this same time, the barrel of brick hit the ground, and the bottom of the barrel fell out. Devoid of the weight of the brick, the barrel weighed approximately fifty pounds.

I refer you again to my weight in block #11. As you might imagine, I began a rather rapid descent down the side of the building.

In the vicinity of the third floor, I met the barrel coming up. This accounts for the fractured ankles and the lacerations of my legs and lower body.

The encounter with the barrel slowed me enough to lessen my injuries when I fell onto the pile of brick, and fortunately only three vertebrae were cracked.

But I am sorry to report that as I lay there in pain on the brick, unable to stand, and watching the empty barrel six stories above me, I once again lost my presence of mind and let go of the rope.

I refer you to the weight of the barrel. With only the rope to impede the descent, the barrel came down, all fifty pounds, and this accounts for the broken ribs and smashed nose.

If you have further questions, you can find me in St. Mary's Hospital still in traction and a body cast.

Sincerely,

Joe the Bricklayer

And whatever you do in word or deed, do all in the name of the Lord Jesus, giving thanks to God the Father through Him (Colossians 3:17).

BUT SERIOUSLY FOLKS: Yes...it just doesn't get much better than this. Pictures in the mind make a story really come alive. In fact, they are better than any TV or DVD!

LET THE CATS OUT...

Another sign you have become a cat person: Your choice of friends depends on whether your cats like them.

Dumb, Dumber, and Dumbest
or Downright Stupidity?

Conklin was on his way home through a dark alley when two thugs attacked him. He fought like a wildcat but was finally overcome and robbed of all the change in his pockets—$1.38 to be exact. "Man, you're quite a fighter," grunted one of the thugs, "but why would you be wanting to put up such a battle for a measly $1.38?"

"Okay," confided Conklin. "I thought you guys wanted the $200 I've got hidden in my shoes!"

The former president of Toyota Motors in Japan planned a memorial that promised to be somewhat less than sublime. He had set aside $445,000 to erect an edifice to honor the people killed in Toyotas throughout the world! (It didn't get built!)

To obtain maximum attention, it's hard to beat a huge mistake!

Being wrong is a human art as old as temple decorations and getting married. No aspect of life has been untouched by this unique capacity. Here are what some people have declared in moments they have regretted:

63

"The Olympic Games can no more have a deficit than a man can have a baby." So said Mayor Jean Drapeau of Montreal three weeks before the 1976 Olympics, as a result of which his city lost one billion dollars!

"The moon has a coating of ice 140 miles thick," stated Hans Horbiger, author of World Ice Theory.

"In all likelihood world inflation is over," said the Director of IMF in 1959.

We should pay a special tribute to Lord Kelvin, president of the Royal Society, 1890–1895, who dogmatically stated the following:

"Radio has no future!"

"Heavier than air flying machines are impossible!"

"X-rays will prove to be a hoax!"

—

Blunders are self-perpetuating. One often begets another. Take the case of the blunderbuss who was dubbed "Wrong Way Corrigan." On July 18, 1938, he took off for a transcontinental flight from New York to Los Angeles. On July 19 he found himself in Dublin, Ireland. Afflicted with terminal understatement, Corrigan said, "It sure does show what a bum navigator a guy can be!"

The second blunder was that the world clamored to make Corrigan an airline pilot. Can't you just hear it now? "This is your captain speaking. There will be a slight delay in your regularly scheduled Seattle to Cleveland flight. Meanwhile, welcome to Nome, Alaska."

During the Middle East War of 1948, Warren Austin, then U.S. Ambassador to the United Nations, in a major speech urged the Arabs and Jews to resolve their disagreements "like good Christians."

—

The following clarification of terms is found in the California State Code of the Division of Consumer Services, Department of Consumer Affairs: "Tenses, Gender, and Number: For the purpose of the rules and regulations contained in this chapter, the present tense includes the past and future tenses, and the future the present; the masculine gender includes the feminine and the feminine the masculine; and the singular includes the plural and the plural the singular." (Huh?)

⌒

Esquire magazine reported in 1963 that Mrs. Agnes Matlock of New Hyde Park, New York, had charged in a lawsuit that her house had burned to the ground while the two fire departments that had answered her call argued over which one had jurisdiction to put out the fire.

⌒

In 1962, some 46,000 Connecticut voters "wrote in" the name of Ted Kennedy for United States Senator. Kennedy was actually running in neighboring Massachusetts!

⌒

Nine Houston firemen confessed to setting a series of fires in southeastern sections of the city to relieve their boredom. One investigator was quoted as saying: "They like to see the red lights and hear the sirens and drive the trucks!"

The Notice to All My Creditors

Dear Creditor:

In reply to your many and insistent requests to send a check to cover my account, I simply wish to inform you that the present condition of my bank account makes it almost impossible to respond.

To wit: my shattered financial conditions are due to federal laws, state laws, county laws, township laws, city laws, corporation laws, liquor laws, tax laws, mothers-in-law, brothers-in-law, sisters-in-law, fathers-in-law, sons-in-law, daughters-in-law, church laws, and various and sundry out-laws!

Through these laws, I am compelled to pay a business tax, amusement tax, head tax, school tax, gas tax (federal, state, county, and city), light tax, water tax, sewer tax, electricity tax, jail tax, employment tax, clothing tax, old-age tax, carpet tacks, liquor tax, cigarette tax, candy tax, federal income tax, state income tax, municipality tax, county tax, road tax, food tax, restaurant tax, furniture tax, street tax, trade-school tax, university tax, community college tax, legislative tax, judicial tax, poor tax, rich tax, garbage tax, car tax, trailer tax, utility tax, service tax, airport tax, RV tax, service tax, tourist tax, and excise tax. Even my brains are taxed.

I am required to get a business license, car license, truck license, trailer license, RV license, boat license, hunting license, fishing license, building license, not to mention a marriage license and dog license and cat license.

I am required to contribute to every society and organization that the genius of man is capable of organizing: to unemployment relief, to flood relief, to hurricane relief, to tornado relief, overseas relief, food relief, blood relief, and to every hospital and charitable institution in this nation, state, county, and city, including the Red Cross, the Purple Cross, the Blue Cross, and of course the Double Cross.

For my own safety I am required to carry life insurance, property insurance, liability insurance, burglar insurance, accident insurance, disability insurance, business insurance, renter's insurance, homeowner's insurance, earthquake insurance, flood insurance, terrorist attack insurance, tornado insurance, lightning insurance, fire insurance, car insurance, RV insurance, pet insurance, old-age insurance, unemployment insurance, jewelry insurance, medical insurance, cancer insurance, gap insurance, supplemental insurance, cell phone insurance, iPad insurance, appliance insurance, and finally umbrella insurance.

My business is so governed that it is no easy matter for me to find out who really owns it. I am inspected, expected, suspected, disrespected, rejected, dejected, examined, re-examined, informed, inspected again, required, summoned, fined, commanded, mistrusted, disavowed, berated, targeted, sued, and compelled until I provide an inexhaustible supply of money for everyone in need, every desire or hope of the human race, not to mention lawyers and Washington politicians!

Simply because I refuse to donate to something or other, I am boycotted, picketed, vilified, lied about, stolen from, gossiped about, held up and held down, not to mention robbed until I am almost ruined, busted, down and out, and in need of sustenance and resuscitation.

I can tell you honestly that except for the miracle that just happened, I could not enclose this check. The wolf that comes to too many doors nowadays came to my door and just had pups in my kitchen, under my table. I promptly sold them, and here is the money you have requested!

With all sincerity,
Yours Truly

"Render therefore to Caesar the things that are Caesar's and to God the things that are God's." But they could not catch Him in His words in the presence of the people. And they marveled at His answer and kept silent (Luke 20:25–26).

BUT SERIOUSLY FOLKS: I'm not even sure that laughing about it makes paying your taxes or bills any more painless. Yes, I know, the only sure things in life are taxes and then finally death. So, as we render unto Caesar the things that are his and render to God the things that are God's, do it with a smile of gratitude as part of the price we have to pay to live in freedom!

LET THE CATS OUT...

If you take your cat in for liposuction surgery—you might be a cat lover.

When God Created Grandchildren and in the Process Created Children!

To those of us who have children in our lives, whether they are our own—grandchildren, nieces, nephews—or neighbor kids or students, the following is something to make you pause.

Whenever these kids are out of control, you can take small comfort from the thought that even God's omnipotence did not extend to His own first two created kids.

After creating heaven and earth and everything in it, God created Adam and Eve, and that's when trouble began.

And the first thing God said to them was "DON'T!"

"Don't what?" Adam replied.

"Don't eat the forbidden fruit," God said.

"Forbidden fruit? We have forbidden fruit? Hey, Eve, we have forbidden fruit!"

"No way!" she enthused.

"Yes way!" he said.

"DO NOT EAT the forbidden fruit!" said God.

"Why?"

"Because I am your Father and Creator and I said SO!" God replied, wondering why He hadn't stopped creating after making elephants, monkeys, giraffes, lions, turkeys, and skunks.

A few days, weeks, or simply minutes later, God saw His children having a "forbidden fruit" break and He was—can I say it?—ticked!

"Didn't I tell you not to eat forbidden fruit?" God asked.

"Uh-huh," through a mouthful Adam replied.

"Then why did you?" asked the Father.

"I don't know...the snake gave me permission," said Eve.

"She started it!" Adam said.

"Did not!"

"Did too!"

"DID NOT!"

"DID TOO!"

"DID NOT, DID NOT!"

"DID TOO, DID TOO!"

Having had it with the two of them at this point, God's punishment was that Adam and Eve should have children of their own. So from time past to time everlasting the pattern has been set for as long as parents, grandparents, and children shall inhabit this earth!

But, perhaps, there is a reassurance in this sad first chapter in human history.

If you have persistently and lovingly attempted to impart wisdom to children and they haven't yet taken it, don't be so hard on yourself. If God had trouble raising His two kids, what makes you think it would be a piece of cake for you?

Before we leave this subject, take another moment to ponder the following:

You spend the first two years of their life teaching them to walk and talk. Then the next sixteen telling them to sit down and be quiet!

Children seldom misquote you. In fact, they usually re-peat word for word what you should not have said or done in the first place!

Behold, children are a heritage from the Lord, the fruit of the womb is a reward. Like arrows in the hand of a war-rior, so are the children of one's youth. Happy is the man [or woman] who has his quiver full of them (Psalm 127:3–5).

BUT SERIOUSLY FOLKS: How about a final bit of ad-vice? Be nice to your kids because they will be taking care of you one day!

LET THE CATS OUT...

Cat person's need-to-know info: Anything that's not attached is a cat toy. Anything that is attached is a scratching post!

Old Age Is Definitely Not for Wimps

The quack was selling a potion at the county fair, which he declared would make a person live to a very ripe old age. "Look at me," he shouted, "hale and hearty. I'm over two hundred years old!"

"Is he really that old?" someone asked the young assistant.

"I can't say," replied the assistant. "I've only worked for him a hundred years."

Since I have retired from life's competition
Each day is filled with complete repetition.
I get up every morning and dust off my wits
Go pick up the paper and read the "obits,"
If my name isn't there I know I'm not dead;
I get a good breakfast and go back to bed.
The reason I know my youth is all spent...
My get-up-and-go has got up and went!

Hardening of the heart makes you grow old faster than hardening of the arteries.

This sign is in front of a small rural cemetery in Tennessee: "As the maintenance of the church cemetery is becoming more costly, it would be appreciated if those who are willing would clip the grass around their own graves."

The seven ages of humans are spills, drills, thrills, bills, ills, pills, and wills!

Believe-It-or-Not!

During a trip to Stockholm, Sweden, Eduardo Sierra, a Spanish Roman Catholic, stopped to pray at a church. The church was empty except for a coffin with the corpse of a man. Sierra prayed in the church for twenty minutes and for the man. Then he signed a condolence book after he saw a note inviting those who prayed for the dead man to enter their names and addresses. He was the first to sign.

Weeks later, Sierra got a call from Stockholm. Jens Svenson, seventy-three, the man in the coffin, turned out to be a real estate tycoon with no close relatives. In his will, Svenson wrote, "Whoever prays for my soul gets all my belongings."

Sierra is now a multimillionaire!

—*The Bild*, Hamburg, Germany

Police were called to help restore order at the Presbyterian Home for the Aged, the scene of a weeklong revolt. Three militant octogenarians were arrested after a scuffle in the north parlor. These three were identified as being leaders of the activist group that seized control of the main parlor three days earlier and had locked the administrator and her staff in a closet.

The leader said the reason for the protest was that, "We have a bunch of young whippersnappers running things around here, and we don't trust anybody under sixty-five."

The second added: "What's the sense of a long life if some fifty-year-old kid is going to tell you what to do?"

The third piped up and said, "We don't have enough action around here!"

Forget about jets, race cars, dragsters, and speed boats. Nothing goes as fast as middle age!

Sarah Adler, noted Jewish actress, never was willing to admit to her actual age. One day a newspaper reporter asked,

"Madam Adler, I don't mean to embarrass you, but would you mind telling me your age?"

Without so much as a pause, she replied, "Sixty-eight."

The reporter objected, "But, Madam, how can that be? I just asked your son Jack his age and he told me he is sixty."

Still undaunted, Sarah replied, "Well, he lives his life and I live mine!"

———

> I can live with my arthritis,
> And my dentures fit me fine.
> I can see with my bifocals
> But I sure do miss my mind.

You Know You're Getting Older When…

- Everything hurts and what doesn't hurt, doesn't work.

- You feel like the morning after the night before and you haven't been anywhere.

- Your little black book contains only names ending in M.D.

- You get winded playing chess or checkers.

- Your children begin to all look middle-aged.

- You join a health club and don't go.

- You decide to procrastinate but never get around to it.

- You know all the answers to life, but nobody asks you the questions.

- You look forward to a dull evening at home.

- You're turning out the lights for economic reasons rather than romantic reasons.

- Your back goes out more often than you do.
- You help a little gray-haired lady cross the street, and she is your wife.
- You've got too much room in your house and not enough in the medicine cabinet.
- You sink your teeth into a juicy T-bone steak and they stay there.

A very wealthy retiree goes into the chic country club with a stunningly beautiful young woman on his arm. After a leisurely lunch, they begin playing tennis. He turns up his pacemaker and the match begins. It's a warm-up. He cranks up his pacemaker, and the second match begins, more intense than the first.

Then they are challenged to a doubles match, and he cranks it up another notch. When the battle get more heated, he cranks up his pacemaker again. Then, suddenly, the old guy slumps to the court, clutching his chest. Their opponents run over and ask the woman, "Want us to call 911?"

She responds, "No, just call AAA. I think they can jump-start him!"

An elderly woman angrily jumped out of her car after a fender bender with another car. "Why can't people ever watch where you're going!" she shouted wildly. "You're the fourth car I've hit this week!"

An older woman slowly, sedately tools her Lincoln Town Car slowly in front of the post office where she was getting ready to parallel park. Before she could begin to back in, a young man in a Miata sports car goes around her, cutting her off, and dove into the spot she was heading for. She rolled her window down and asks, "Why?"

He replies, "Because I'm young and quick!" And he runs into the post office.

When he comes out, he sees that she had pulled ahead of him and in the midst of backing into the next space, she began backing up a little too forcefully and rams into his poor little sports car, reducing it to rubble. He loses it and shouts at her, "WHY?"

She smiles broadly. "Because I'm old and rich!"

The "B.C."

There happen to be a whole lot of versions to this little story, and the original source has long since been lost to antiquity. This, however, should not stop us from enjoying it one more time! So here goes...

My friend is a rather old-fashioned lady, quite elegant and delicate, especially in her use of language. She and her husband were planning on a weeklong camping trip, so she wrote an e-mail to a particular campground to make reservations. However, she didn't quite know how to ask about toilet facilities. She didn't want to write "toilet" in her correspondence. After much deliberation, she thought of the very old-fashioned term Bathroom Commode. But when she typed it in, she thought she was being a bit too forward, so she rewrote the entire request and referred to bathroom commode as the "B.C." She wrote, "Does your campground have its own B.C.?"

Well, the campground owner was an up-to-date modern guy and couldn't figure out what she was asking. This "B.C." business had him stumped. He asked some of the other campers if they knew what the B.C. was and none of them knew. So he finally decided that she must be asking about the location for the local Baptist Church, so he wrote the following e-mail:

Dear Madam:
I regret very much the delay in answering your e-mail but I now take the pleasure of informing you that yes, we have a B.C. and it is located six miles north of the campground. It is capable of seating about 250 people at one time. I will admit that it is quite a distance away if you are in the habit of going regularly. No doubt you will be pleased to know that a great number of people take their lunches along and make a day of

it. The last time my wife and I went was six months ago, and it was so crowded that we had to stand up the whole time.

Right now, there is a supper planned to raise money for more seats. It will be held in the basement of the B.C. I would like to say that it pains me that I am not able to go more regularly, but it is not for lack of desire on my part. As we grow older, it seems to be more of an effort, especially in cold weather.

If you do decide to come to our campground, perhaps I could go with you the first time that you go, sit with you, and introduce you to all the other folks. Remember, that this is a very friendly community.

Sincerely,
The Campground Owner

A merry heart does good, like medicine, but a broken spirit dries the bones (Proverbs 17:22).

BUT SERIOUSLY FOLKS: Oh well...what more can be added other than to tell you that it's okay to share a good, old-fashioned belly laugh! A good laugh works better than a dose of medication because the Good Book told us so!

LET THE CATS OUT...
Cat's modus operandi: If you can't get anyone's attention, paw their computer keyboard until you do.

Jokes from Around the World

FROM ENGLAND

Who among us will claim the British have no sense of humor? The British Association of the Advancement of Science issued a challenge: "Help us identify the world's funniest joke."

They got some help. More than ten thousand jokes were submitted at the Association's website, and more than a hundred thousand people from seventy countries cast votes to select the winner.

The following is the joke that came out on top, as reported by *Reuters* and other news services:

The fictional British detective Sherlock Holmes and his associate, Doctor Watson, are camping in the woods. They pitch a tent and go to sleep. Later, Holmes abruptly wakes up Watson.

HOLMES: "Watson, look up at the stars and tell me what you deduce."

WATSON: "I see millions of stars, and if there are millions of stars, and if even a few of those have planets, it is quite likely there are some planets like Earth. And if there are a few planets like Earth out there, there might also be life."

HOLMES: "Watson, you idiot! Somebody stole our tent!"

If this is really the world's funniest joke, then we're all in trouble. Do you think you could top this?

READER'S DIGEST—Leader of the Pack!

Humor is a powerful way to cope with life and many of the circumstances beyond our control, so it's important to us. *Reader's Digest* must have picked up on this early on. They claim they have been sent more than twenty million jokes and have published more than 100,000 of them. Would you call them experts in joke evaluation?

The various language editions of *Reader's Digest* did a search for the funniest jokes and came up with the following selections. (Some of these may sound familiar, thanks to the ever-present Internet.)

FROM BRAZIL

Tired of waiting in the back of the line to get on Noah's ark, a flea jumps from one animal to another as she moves closer to the front. She leaps and leaps until she lands on the back of an elephant. The pachyderm turns to its mate and says testily, "I knew it! Here they go with the pushing and shoving!"

FROM CANADA

A man says to a friend, "My wife is on a three-week diet."
"Oh yeah? How much has she lost so far?"
"Two weeks."

FROM FINLAND

Hannu wants everything to be perfect for his anniversary trip to the hotel where he and his wife honeymooned thirty years earlier. So he gets there a day early to make all the arrangements. That night he e-mails her but misspells the address, and it goes to a recent widow.

The next day, the widow's son finds his mother passed out in front of her computer. On the screen is this e-mail: "My darling wife, I've just gotten here and everything's set for your arrival tomorrow. I hope your trip down here will be as pleasant as mine. P.S.: It's really hot!"

FROM IRELAND

Two bricklayers were working on a building. Their super-intendent paused to ask precisely what they were building. The more stolid bricklayer replied, "I don't care, and I don't know. All I do is slap this crummy mortar on these crummy bricks and pile them up in a crummy line."

The second and more imaginative bricklayer enthused, "I'm building a great cathedral with a beautiful spire that will point straight up to heaven."

The second man was fired because they were building a garage.

FROM ISRAEL

An Israeli diplomat tells about a duck that was preparing to paddle across the Suez Canal when a scorpion appeared with a bag of grain and said, "All this is yours if you will let me ride across on your back."

"My mother always warned me to beware of the treachery of scorpions," demurred the duck. "How do I know you won't sting me in midstream?"

"Silly duck," scoffed the scorpion. "In that case wouldn't we both drown?"

So the duck said, "Hop aboard," but sure enough, halfway across the canal the scorpion stung it. As they both went down, the duck gasped, "What made you do it?"

The scorpion gasped back, "What else could you expect? This is the Middle East."

FROM POLAND

Nearing the end, Stanislaw is surrounded by loved ones. As the final moment approaches, he gathers all his strength and whispers, "I must tell you my greatest secret."

His family urges him on. "Before I got married I had it all," Stanislaw explains. "Fast cars, cute girls, plenty of money. But a good friend warned me, 'Get married and start a family. Otherwise, no one will be there to give you a glass of water to drink when you're on your death bed.' So I took his advice, I traded the girls for a wife, booze for baby food. I sold my Ferrari and invested in college funds. And now here we are. And you know what?"

"What?"

"I'm not even thirsty!"

FROM RUSSIA

Due to the recession, to save on energy costs, the light at the end of the tunnel will be turned off. —God

FROM SERBIA

A neighbor finds a young boy sitting on the stairs crying. "What's the matter, honey?" she asks him.

"It's my father," the boy sobs. "He hit his finger with a hammer."

"Why are you crying?"

"Because first I laughed."

It's interesting that Russians prefer dark humor, while we Americans go for the big laugh, but the Brits want theirs to be dry. The bottom line is, what we laugh at says a whole lot about who we are in this world. So let's all laugh together!

The Alternate Medical Dictionary...Condensed

Due to the controversy and the many changes in the medical and health care fields, it will be necessary for all persons contacting physicians or hospitals to become familiar with the following medial terms. Since we have been talking about the medical benefits that can be yours through a life filled with laughter, you will discover a further enhancement with a new understanding of what you will be facing when confronting these new medical-professional terminologies.

ARTERY: the study of paintings in an art gallery
BACTERIA: the back door of a typical cafeteria
BARIUM: what doctors do when one of their patients dies
BOWEL: a letter sort of like an a, e, i, o, u, or sometimes y
BENIGN: what you are after you be eight
CAESARIAN SECTION: a neighborhood or part of the city of Rome, Italy
CAT SCAN: searching for a lost cat
COLIC: a very wet sheep dog
D & C: where Washington is located as the capital of the United States
DILATE: to live a whole lot longer, as opposed to di-soon
ENEMA: not a friendly friend, someone who wants you dead
FESTER: a whole lot quicker than just being fast

G.I. SERIES: a bunch of military ball games
HANGNAIL: a simple, single coat hook
LABOR PAINS: when you get hurt at work
MAMMOGRAM: a telegram or e-mail to your own mama
MINOR OPERATION: digging for coal in a small mine
MORBID: waiting for a higher offer
NITRATES: really, quite a bit cheaper than day rates
NODE: when you was made aware of something
OUTPATIENT: a person who has fainted dead away
PAP SMEAR: a special fatherhood kind of test
PELVIS: a first or second cousin to Elvis
POSTOPERATIVE: a letter carrier for the U.S. Postal Service
SECRETION: trying to hide something from other persons
SEIZURE: some kind of an ancient Roman emperor
TABLET: a rather small table

TERMINAL SICKNESS: when you get sick at the airport
TUMOR: an extra pair of anything

ULTRASOUND: a very loud, loud sound, like ultimate
VEIN: a person who is very conceited
URINE: the opposite of being out
VARICOSE VEINS: veins that are very close together

PLEASE NOTE: SUCH TERMINOLOGY
SHALL BE IN COMMON USE UNTIL THE
NEXT BULLETIN UPDATE FROM THE U.S.
SURGEON GENERAL!

The late Pastor Bill Popejoy, a pastor in Belton, Missouri, was known for his whimsical way of stating things. Yet he too experienced some tough times in dealing with cancer. Among these problems, he shared this experience of facing surgery for cancer of the throat. As he prayed, he said the devil tempted him with the words, "You're going to die!"

In response, he said, "Wonderful! That means I'm going to heaven sooner!"

Then the tempter said, "You're going to lose your voice."

To which God prompted Popejoy to say, "God is giving me a ministry of writing."

Once more came the attack: "You will be deformed in your face!"

The answer was, "I've already looked in the mirror!"

Then Pastor Popejoy concluded with his version of this Bible verse from the Book of James: "Laugh at the devil and he will flee from you!" And in the final words of Pastor Bill: "A LAUGH A DAY WILL KEEP THE DEVIL AWAY!"

The thief does not come except to steal, and to kill, and to destroy. I have come that they [YOU] may have life, and that they [YOU] may have it more abundantly (John 10:10).

BUT SERIOUSLY FOLKS: Humor is a powerful tool against all kinds of human ailments—physical as well psychological. The enemy who seeks to destroy you can tolerate your promises, dodge your rebukes, and listen to your prayers of unbelief, but laughter is something he has not heard very much of from the Church and the people of the Church.

LET THE CATS OUT...

"Cats are smarter than dogs. You can't get eight cats to pull a sled through snow." —*Jeff Valdez*

Football-Speak Theology

In the never-ceasing effort to attract the unchurched and to attempt to cross the bridge to football fans who don't frequent a church as often as a football game, this is to prove that a certain kind of understanding of interests outside the church can also have an application inside the church. You may want to learn these theological terms and intersperse these with your friends whom you might take to church with you.

Sorry, these aren't necessarily good football or good theology. But then again, it might be better just to be able to express something now and then, intelligent or not, especially during the everlasting football season. But then again, it just might impress your football-crazed friends that you know the terminology. Here goes, enjoy and memorize until these become second nature:

DRAFT CHOICE: The decision to sit close to the heating vent in the wintertime and the air-conditioning vents in the summertime.

PASS INTERFERENCE: What Mama does with her eyes when she sees son Jimmy writing notes or text-messaging to friends while in church.

TWO-MINUTE WARNING: The chairman of the church board sitting on a front pew, taking a very long look at his watch in full view of the preacher, especially as the clock approaches high noon.

FUMBLE: One very long, boring, and lousy sermon.

QUARTERBACK: What church members, who happen to believe that religion is free, want after putting their weekly $1 in the offering plate.

PASSING GAME: What ushers do with the offering plate each Sunday morning and evening and Wednesday night.

CORNERBACKS: These are the people who always occupy the back pews, always on the outside aisle, so as to defend their space or favorite pew.

ILLEGAL MOTION: Leaving before the sermon is finished or the final benediction has been pronounced.

PENALTY: What the church gets when its members stay home with their wallets or purses or checkbooks.

HOLDING PENALTY: What the ushers attempt to do to those who run out of and back into the sanctuary several times on the excuse of potty breaks, drink breaks, cell phone breaks, baby-changing breaks, etc.

END RUN: Any child who successfully escapes both parents and all the ushers on his way out of the church service.

FAIR CATCH: Holding the offering plate in front of each attendee until money is placed in it.

CLIPPING: What the resident, self-appointed church historian is always doing, just for the sake of the historical record.

HALF-BACK: What the choir, seated behind or beside the preacher, sees while the sermon is being delivered.

NOSE GUARD: What a nursery worker wears during the cold and flu season among their little charges.

SUPER BOWL CHAMP: Any church that actually is doing the will of God.

FINAL GUN: The closing benediction!

—Thanks to *William Ellis and Earl Banning*, Religious Broadcasting, 1/93, selected, condensed, and modified

He will surely turn violently and toss you like a ball... (Isaiah 22:18).

BUT SERIOUSLY FOLKS: Football is a game in which 70,000 fans who are desperately in need of exercise watch twenty-two guys who desperately are in need of rest. Church is much like that too, unfortunately for many. In your case, is church a spectator sport, or are you an active participant?

LET THE CATS OUT...

Cat philosophy of life: When you get into trouble, purr and look cute.

From the Wild, Wild World of Sports

Once, not so very long ago, a scared football team from a Southern California university (which shall remain unnamed) invaded the home field of the mighty fighting Irish of Notre Dame University to do battle with the powerful Irish team and the ghosts of the past. It promised to be an intimidating game for the visiting team. Obviously, the visiting coach had a problem, as the Irish were a four touchdown favorite. This coach was attempting to bring his wretched team up for the game, but no amount of pep talk seemed to inspire his over-matched team. They were terrified of their prospects.

Finally in desperation, in his last-minute talk just before they were to take the field, he said, "Sure, we'll get trimmed, but let's show all those people out there we really know what we are doing! Let's go get them! Let's start our run from this locker room and have a full head of steam as we reach the stadium entrance!"

Then he threw open the door of the locker room and the inspired football squad dashed out at a mad run, and all forty of them ran smack-dab into the Notre Dame swimming pool! The coach had opened the wrong door!

Folks...it just doesn't get much better than that! I only wish I had been there! But the mental picture is fabulous!

Now we bring you, unabridged, some quotable quotes directly from the exciting wide, wide world of sports!

LEE TREVINO: On the rough at the Royal Birkdale golf course, site of the British Open tournament: "At the fifteenth hole, we put down my bag to hunt for the ball. Found the ball, lost the bag!"

JIM VALVANO: Former North Carolina State basketball coach: "I don't like all those TV time-outs. I run out of things to say to my team."

WILLIAM PERRY: Also known as "The Refrigerator" because of his huge size, was a Clemson University defensive guard, on the two-year TV and post-season ban imposed on the Tigers by the NCAA: "What makes it hard is that we can't watch television for two years."

MICKEY RIVERS: A former Yankee baseball player, then Rangers player, denying he'd have problems with Yankee owner George Steinbrenner or manager Billy Martin if, as rumored, he returned to the Yankees: "Me and George and Billy are two of a kind."

JOHN BUTCHER: Pitcher with the Rangers after tossing a one-hit game: "I threw about 90 percent fastballs and sliders, 50 percent fastballs, 50 percent sliders...wait, I'm starting to sound like Mickey Rivers."

ED CROAKE: New York Giants football team public relations man, on the 329-pound defensive end Leonard

Marshall: "We put him on a Cambridge diet, and he ate half of Cambridge."

DON MATTHEWS: Coach of the Canadian Football League's British Columbia Lions, asked whether his team would attempt any quick kicks in an upcoming game in Vancouver's domed stadium: "Only when we have the air-conditioning at our backs."

DON OTT: Who was then a member of the Evangelical Athletes in Action basketball team, explaining his club's twenty-nine-point loss to UCLA after defeating ORU (Oral Roberts University) by twenty-nine points in its previous game: "You might say they did unto us as we did unto others. My football team is playing such lousy ball, I had left three tickets in my locked car. Someone broke in and left three more."

YOGI BERRA: "Baseball is 90 percent mental. The other half is physical."

MICHAEL JORDAN: One of the best basketball players to play the game, one time he scored sixty-nine points. The coach put in a substitute to finish the game, and he scored one point. The media asked the sub later, "What is the most important game of your life?"

He replied, "The game when Michael Jordan and I scored seventy points in one game!"

Did you hear about the track coach who put in the cross-eyed discus thrower, not to set any records, but to keep the crowd alert!

Any baseball team could sure use a man who plays every position superbly, who never strikes out, and who never makes an error. But there's no way for the manager to make him lay down his hot dog and come out of the grandstand.

—

The college football coach called practice to a halt to "chew out" one of his huge freshman tackles for making a stupid play. Head bowed, the monster tackle stood in silence as the coach called him every kind of a name, topping off the blast with, "What's your IQ anyway?"

Startled, the tackle looked up, thought a moment, and said: "Twenty-twenty!"

—

A football coach was asked by a fellow coach how he picked out a team from a bunch of raw recruits. "I hate to give away my secrets," he replied, "but I'll tell you. I take them out into the woods. Then at a given signal, I start them running. Those that run around the trees are chosen as guards. Those that run into the trees are chosen as tackles."

—

What Has Happened to Murphy's Law?

I remind you, if you haven't already forgotten it, that "Murphy's Law" says: "IF ANYTHING CAN GO WRONG, IT WILL." It has been assumed this law was the prime operational scheme at work in understanding the latter half of the twentieth century. However, we are now living in a new century, and some further research has been done. I now present to you some selected restatements, corollaries, and revisions to the basic law, up to and including this from Gerald Manning of Cork, Ireland:

Gerald's Meta-Murphic Law: Murphy's Law does not apply to Murphy's Law.

Corollary: If Murphy's Law could go wrong, it would, but it can't so it doesn't.

When stated like that (read above), the law begins to have problems. There is at least a crack in a law that doesn't obey itself. It would be like allowing the Law of Gravity to apply to all people except Sir Isaac Newton.

However, there is good news. Increasing evidence is mounting that Murphy's Law is not infallible. This concept is put into words by "Cleve" Bishop of Littleton, Colorado, who wrote:

Bishop's Revision: When you count on Murphy's Law to work, it doesn't.

But this is a radical revision that had previously been postulated in the form of:

Law of Murphy's Law's Self-Application: Onesimo T. Almeida postulated that if Murphy's Law can go wrong, it will go wrong exactly when you need or want it to show its accuracy.

And there is...**Gayer's Amendment to Murphy's Law:** Anything that can go wrong will go wrong except at the repair shop, where it will magically, mysteriously, and temporarily repair itself. Once outside of said repair shop, refer once again to Murphy's Law.

But there is a positive **corollary** of this: **Osgood's Exception:** Whatever can go right, might!

This was stated by radio commentator Charles Osgood after telling the story of a family that had unwittingly stored four bottles of nitroglycerin on a shelf in their basement for forty-one years without incident. This stuff could have easily been set off by a jolt or bump. When the bottles were discovered and consequently destroyed by a police bomb squad, it was estimated that there was enough power in them to have destroyed several city blocks!

But then again, there is more to this. What we are witnessing is not an exception or two, but a serious flaw: Murphy's Law applies to Murphy's Flaw, which is expressed like this:

Murphy's Flaw: If anything can't go wrong (i.e., Murphy's Law), it will.

However, this must give way to **Fetridge's Law:** Important things that are supposed to happen do not happen, especially when people are looking.

This little known law was named by and for Claude Fetridge, an engineer working for NBC radio, who in 1936 came up with the idea of a live broadcast to report on the departure of the swallows from their roost at Mission San Juan Capistrano on St. John's Day, October 23. Fetridge's equipment-laden, hardworking crew arrived to find that the swallows had left a day early on October 22, something that had not happened in the last hundred years of the swallows' timely departures!

If you understand all that I've just written, you must have missed something. Read it again, because if MURPHY'S LAW had not been suspended, this book would have never seen the light of day or appeared in print!

"Vanity of vanities," says the Preacher; "Vanity of vanities, all is vanity." What profit has a man from all his labor in which he toils under the sun? (Eccl. 1:2–3).

BUT SERIOUSLY FOLKS: What more can I say? Not much...other than to give you **DiGiovanni's Law,** which states that the number of "laws" will expand only enough to fill the publishing space available!

LET THE CATS OUT...
Fact of life: Cats don't own people. They prefer a lease option.

Just More Jokes
for the Fun of It

A man was walking along a California beach and was in deep prayer to the Lord. He said, "Lord, You have promised to give me the desires of my heart. That's what I am asking You for right now! Please give me a confirmation that You will grant this."

Suddenly, the sky clouded up over his head and the Lord, in a booming voice, spoke to him, "I have searched your heart and determined it to be pure in motive. The last time I issued a blank wish request, it was to Solomon. He didn't disappoint me with his request for wisdom. I think I can trust that you won't disappoint me either. Because you have been faithful to Me in all ways, I will grant you one wish you ask for."

The man sat and thought a while, then said, "I've always wanted to go to Hawaii, but I'm deadly afraid of flying and I get very seasick on a ship. Could you build a bridge to Hawaii, so I can drive over there to visit whenever I want?"

The Lord laughed and said, "That's impossible! Think of the logistics of that! How would the supports ever reach the floor of the Pacific? Think of how much concrete and how much steel! Your request is very materialistic, a little disappointing, and a little selfish. I could do it, but it's hard for Me to justify your craving for worldly things. Take a little more time and think of another wish, a request you think would honor and glorify Me as well."

The man thought about it and finally said, "Here's the deal, Lord. I've been married and divorced four times. My wives always said that I don't care about them and that I'm insensitive. So I wish that I could understand women. I want to know how they feel inside and what they're thinking when they give me the silent treatment...I want to know why they're crying...I want to know what they really mean when they say 'nothing'...I want to know how to make them truly happy. That's the wish that I want, Lord."

After a few moments, God replied, "About that bridge, do you want two lanes or four?"

The richest man in town was moved emotionally by the church service, and he stood and asked to speak a word to the congregation, which the pastor granted.

He said, "I remember the day I earned my very first dollar. That night I went to church and the speaker told about his missions work. I had only that single dollar, and I felt I had to make a decision: Give it to God's worthy cause or keep it for myself. I gave the missionary, God's man, all that I had. I believe God blessed my decision so much that I am a multimillionaire today!"

As he sat down, a little old woman shouted, "I dare you to do it again!"

OLD LAWYERS...never die; they just lose their appeals!

OLD MUSICIANS...never die; they just get played out!

OLD PREACHERS...never die; they just say the final benediction!

OLD GOLFERS...never die; they just hit the rough!

101

OLD GARBAGE COLLECTORS...never die; they just hit the dumps!

OLD TEACHERS...never die; they just lose their lesson plans!

OLD JOKES...never die; they just get recycled!

WALT DISNEY...never died; he's in suspended animation!

OLD ACCOUNTANTS...never die; they just lose their balance!

One man was telling his friend about his wife being in labor with their first child. Things were going pretty well, she did her breathing and he helped...then suddenly, she began shouting: "Shouldn't...couldn't...didn't...can't...won't!"

"Doctor, what's wrong with my wife?"

"Nothing. She's just having a lot of contractions!"

Question: How many egomaniacs does it take to change a lightbulb?

Answer: Only one. The egomaniac holds the lightbulb while the rest of the world revolves around him.

Do you know what you get when you play a country song backward? You get your job back, you get your house back, you get your horse back, your wife back, your pickup truck back...and a whole lot more!

Why did the cowboy buy a dachshund? He was told to get-a-long-little-doggy!

As a crowded airliner prepared to take off, the silence was shattered by a five-year-old boy who picked that moment to throw a temper tantrum. No matter what his very frustrated, embarrassed mother did to calm him, he continued to scream and kick the seats around him. Suddenly from the back of the plane, an older man in the uniform of an Air Force General walked up and stopped the flustered mother with an upraised hand. The white-haired, courtly, soft-spoken general leaned down, motioned toward his chest, and whispered something into the boy's ear.

The boy instantly calmed down, took his mother's hand, and quickly fastened his seat belt. All was instantly quiet and the passengers burst into applause.

As the general went back to his seat, a cabin attendant asked, "Excuse me, General. Could I ask you what magic words you used on that little boy?"

The general smiled and confided, "I showed him my pilot's wings, service stars, and battle ribbons, and explained that they entitled me to throw one passenger out of the plane's door on any flight I would so choose."

Teacher: "Willy, name one important thing we have today that we didn't have ten years ago."

Willy: "Me!"

A very faithful religious man who reached the ripe old age of 105 suddenly stopped attending the synagogue. Alarmed by the aged man's absence after so many years of faithful attendance, the rabbi visited the venerable congregant. "Why after all these years do we not see you at our services?"

"I'll tell you, rabbi, when I reached 105 I figured God must have forgotten about me, and I don't want to remind Him."

An African chieftain's daughter was offered as a bride to the son of a neighboring potentate in exchange for two cows and four sheep. It was agreed that the big swap was to be effected on the shore of the swift-flowing stream that separated the tribes. Pop and his daughter showed up at the appointed time on one side of the stream only to discover that the bridegroom and his livestock were waiting on the other side.

"Stupid fool," grunted the father of the bride. "He doesn't seem to know which side his bride is bartered on."

One Hunter's Recollection of the First Day of Elk Hunting Season

2:00 a.m.: Alarm clock rings! I hit the snooze button.

3:00 a.m.: Hunting partners arrive, drag me out of bed! Throw everything, including the kitchen sink, in pickup.

3:30 a.m.: Leave for the deep woods and beautiful back country and mountains.

5:00 a.m.: Furiously drive back home, alone, to pick up my gun and license. Drive like mad to get back before daylight.

6:30 a.m.: Set up my camp. Forgot the tent!

7:00 a.m.: Head into the deep woods, late. Spot eight elk moving toward me at a brisk clip. Now within range.

7:37 a.m.: Take careful aim at lead bull, hold breath, great rack, gently squeeze trigger. Click!

7:38 a.m.: Frantically load gun while watching trophy bull and seven elk go over hill.

9:30 a.m.: Head back to camp for coffee break.

10:00 a.m.: Still looking for camp. Realize I don't know where camp is!

11:58 a.m.: Fire three shots, the signal for help. Notice wild berries, eat wild berries.

12:05 p.m.: Fire three more shots. Run out of shells. Eight elk come back!

12:45 p.m.: Strange feeling in stomach. Realize I must have eaten poisoned berries!

1:35 p.m.: Rescued! They rush me to nearest hospital to get stomach pumped.

3:30 p.m.: Arrive back in camp. Leave camp to go after eight elk, again.

3:50 p.m.: Return back to camp for shells. Load gun. Leave camp again.

4:30 p.m.: Empty gun on squirrel that is bugging me. Miss every shot!

5:00 p.m.: Arrive back in camp. See eight elk grazing right near camp!

5:01 p.m.: Load gun. Fire gun. One dead pickup!

5:35 p.m.: Hunting partners arrive back in camp, both dragging elk.

5:36 p.m.: Repress desire to shoot hunting partners! Stumble and fall into campfire.

6:00 p.m.: Change clothes, throw burned ones into campfire.

6:05 p.m.: Take pickup, leave hunting partners and elk in camp. Pickup boils over, caused because of hole in radiator!

6:16 p.m.: Start walking. Stumble and fall, again, drop gun into mud.

6:25 p.m.: Meet bear! Take aim. Fire gun. Blow up barrel plugged with mud!

6:26 p.m.: Run fast, run very fast! Climb nearest tree, bear climbs, climb higher, bear stops climb and returns to ground.

6:29 p.m.: Bear continues to circle below tree!

7:30 p.m.: Holler very loud for hunting partners. Too far away, they can't hear!

8:49 p.m.: Bear still circles, growling all the time!

9:38 p.m.: Bear finally leaves, walking into deep woods.

9:46 p.m.: Very cautiously climb down. Wrap gun around tree!

10:18 p.m.: Finally hitchhike a ride with farmer to town.

11:49 p.m.: Home at last!

12:15 noon the next day: Watch football game on TV, slowly tearing up hunting license into very small pieces, place pieces in envelop, then mail it to the game and fish department with detailed instructions on what to do with it!

> *"Behold, I will send for many fishermen," says the Lord, "and they shall fish them; and afterward I will send for many hunters, and they shall hunt them from every mountain and every hill, and out of the holes of the rocks"* (Jeremiah 16:16).

BUT SERIOUSLY FOLKS: Humor can and should be found in every kind of human endeavor. And the Bible encourages us to "give thanks in everything." Notice, it doesn't say "for everything give thanks." We can rejoice in it but perhaps not for it! And yes, thankfully, life does go on!

LET THE CATS OUT...

Another sign you may have become a cat person: Your friends don't ask how you are; they ask how your cats are doing.

Momma Don't 'Low No Ethnic Jokes Here

Did you hear about the preacher who told his congregation one Sunday morning, "Folks, I've been thinking about this and feel bad. We have been telling too many ethnic jokes, and when doing this, have offended lots of people: the Swedes, the Russians, the Poles, and so on. You catch my thinking. From now on if you must tell an ethnic joke, tell it about the Hittites because they are a group of people who no longer exist. In this way you will no longer offend anybody who is alive today."

The following Sunday morning, the pastor began his sermon, "There were these two Hittites named Ole and Sven."

Englishman: "Do you enjoy Kipling?"
Norwegian: "I don't know...I've never kippled."

Phone rings.
Hittite answers: "Sure is." Hangs up.
Wife: "Who was it?"
Hittite: "I don't know. Someone said, 'Long distance from New York.' So I said, 'Sure is.'"

The Hittites are planning to launch a space flight to the sun. When asked by a reporter how they planned to avoid burning up, a Hittite spokesperson answered, "We figure on going at night."

How do you get a one-armed Hittite out of a tree?
You wave at him.

Did you hear about the Hittite who received a new boomerang for his birthday? He went crazy trying to throw away the old one!

The Hittites in our community are so smart they have finally figured out that they can also turn right on green!

The Hittite next door is teaching his Golden Labrador dog to jump out of an airplane with a parachute. He calls him "Sky Lab."

Why did the Hittite have the strong urge to hit a laughing spiritualist? Because he always wanted to strike a happy medium.

So...you don't believe Hittites are athletic? My cousin was the javelin catcher in the last Olympics!

What's the happiest five years of a Hittite's life? First grade.

The space program of a certain unnamed country sent a monkey and a Hittite on a space flight. The monkey's job was to perform certain scientific routines, pushing levers, punching buttons, reading dials, etc. The Hittite's job was to feed the monkey.

The Hittite was asked, "What do Eric the Red and Smokey the Bear have in common?"
The answer: "They both have the same middle name."

Two Hittites were hunting ducks. At the end of the day, they'd had no luck. One turned to the other and asked, "Do you think maybe we haven't been throwing the dog high enough?"

A Hittite and two others were sentenced to death by firing squad. The firing squad aimed their rifles, and one of the prisoners was asked if he had any last words. He shouted at the top of his lungs, "Tornado!" Everyone scattered and ran for cover. When order was restored, they found he had escaped.

The next victim was lined up, rifles were made ready, and he was asked if he had any last words. He shouted, "Earthquake! Earthquake!" Everyone dove for safety and this man escaped, as well. Order was restored and...

The Hittite was brought in front of the firing squad and he was asked if he had any final words. So he yelled, "Fire!" and they did!

———

Did you hear about the Hittite who received cufflinks and a short-sleeved shirt for his birthday? So he had his wrists pierced!

———

This Hittite says that his wife will buy anything that's marked down. Last week, she purchased an escalator.

———

The Hittite showed up for work with bandaged ears. "What happened?" asked a fellow worker.

"Well," said the Hittite. "Last night I was ironing my shirt when the phone rang and I picked up the iron by mistake."

"Well, what happened to the other ear?" asked his friend.

"Oh, that. Well, I had to call the doctor."

———

A farmer, upon hearing that a bunch of Hittites would be hunting in the area of his farm, took a paint brush and painted Horse...Cow...Pig on his farm animals. Well, these Hittite hunters managed to hunt without shooting an animal, but they riddled the farmer's tractor with the following name plate on it: John Deere!

—

This particular Hittite wasn't too smart, but he managed to make a fine living buying and selling used cars. He'd buy a car for $1,000 and sell it for $4,000. For example, he explained, "I ain't too good at figures, but I'm satisfied with a three percent profit."

—

Seniors Who Laugh...
Will Last and Last and Last and Last...

After forty years of married life, a woman's husband died. For several months she sat alone in her home. Finally, she decided to do something about her loneliness. She went to a pet store and looked at snakes, gerbils, fish, birds, dogs, and cats, but nothing seemed to be just right for her. Finally the owner showed her one of his prized parrots.

"Does it talk?"

"Absolutely...a real chatterbox. Friendly disposition and a wide vocabulary. That is why this parrot is so expensive," replied the owner.

"Sold." She bought it and a large elegant cage. At last a companion! Perfect! But when she got the bird home, it didn't say a word. She went back to the store and complained, "Not a word! I can't get a sound out of the bird! I'm worried."

"Well, you need to buy a mirror. A parrot needs a mirror so that while looking at himself, he'll talk." So she bought a mirror. Time passed, another week, no words. Back to the pet store, again.

"The parrot isn't talking, even with the mirror."

"Did you buy a ladder?"

"No, I didn't think it needed a ladder." So she bought a ladder. Another week, no words. The next time it was a bell...then a swing, more silence. No talk.

Suddenly, one day, she burst into the pet store and this time she was really steamed. The owner met her and asked, "How's the parrot? I'll bet—"

She cut him off, "It died!" My expensive bird is dead at the bottom of the cage with a mirror, bell, ladder, and swing!" Was she ever mad!

He said, "Well, I just can't believe that. I'm shocked. Did it ever say anything at all?"

"Well, yes, as a matter of fact it did. As it lay there taking its last few breaths, it said very faintly, 'Don't they have any food down at that pet store?'"

It's so easy in this world to have our focus blurred and lose our way. We've missed what this life is all about. As we learn how to rejoice, relax, and rest, we discover that the Giver of Life relieves, renews, and restores.

Norman Cousins wrote a book entitled *Anatomy of an Illness as Perceived by the Patient*. In it he talks about his battle with an "incurable" disease, and the pain he endured as his body's collagen was deteriorating (the fibrous material that holds your body's cells together). In Cousin's own words, he was "becoming unstuck."

He took matters into his own hands and began treating himself, with his doctor's approval, by 1) taking vitamins, 2) eating only healthy food, and 3) undergoing "laugh therapy." He did this by watching old Marx Brothers movies, clips from Candid Camera, films from The Three Stooges, and cartoons for kids (especially the "Road Runner" ones), and he read anything or watched anything else that would make him laugh.

He found that if he could laugh hard for ten minutes, he could get two hours of relief from pain. Cousins recovered and lived many years beyond the medical folks' expectations and predictions. He literally cured himself through laughter therapy! He started something that is currently under study as to the therapeutic effects on health and longevity.

The Bible was correct...once again! The New King James Version of Proverbs 15:15 says, "He who is of a merry heart has a continual feast!"

"These things I have spoken to you, that My joy may remain in you, and that your joy may be full" (John 15:11).

BUT SERIOUSLY FOLKS: Think of the impact we can have as future citizens of heaven, as we live joyful, hilariously enjoyable, responsible, yet wonderfully carefree lives among people who cannot seem to find anything funny or humorous about life!

LET THE CATS OUT...
If you insist that callers say a few words to your cat—you might be a cat lover.

Out of the Mouths
of Grandbabes

The Sunday school teacher asked a little boy to define a "lie." He responded: "It is an abomination unto the Lord and a very present help in the time of need."

—

The Children's Church was canceled one Sunday morning due to the illness of the two ladies in charge. The children were then kept in the adult main service. Little Johnny got overly tired during the too-long sermon. After a lot of squirming, he finally asked his mother in a stage whisper so all nearby could hear: "If we give him the money now, Mom, will he let us out?"

—

The visiting preacher kept using the word *procrastination* in his sermon. After the service, a little girl asked, "What does the preacher mean when he says 'procrastination'?"

The patient mother responded, "What do you think it means?"

The daughter said, "It must be one of our church doctrines."

—

Arthur Arnold, a traveling evangelist known for his mastery of the Old Testament, shared what happened when he was invited to a home for dinner. Before leaving the house, he asked the family if they wanted him to read a special portion of the Bible to them. The lady of the home said to her young son, "Go bring the big book we read out of so much."

The little guy returned with the current Sears and Roebuck catalog!

⎯

The following question was popped in a Sunday school class of sixth-graders: "What are the sins of omission?"

One boy volunteered, "Those are the sins we should have committed and didn't."

⎯

The Christmas program had been beautiful and everyone had had a lovely evening at the local Los Angeles Nazarene Church. The emcee ended the evening nicely as he announced that their soloist, "the young and talented Cherilee would close the evening 'Away in a Manger' with the men's chorus."

⎯

"Who led the children of Israel across the Red Sea?" asked the teacher and got no response. She then pointed to a new boy in class and asked him. He replied, "It sure wasn't me. We just moved here from Ohio."

⎯

The pastor was speaking on the story of the Good Samaritan. He paused and asked, "Now, children, what would you do if you saw a man beaten and bleeding and lying in the gutter?"

A little voice from the second row quickly responded, "Oooo...I'd throw up!"

A teacher asked her class, "Are you all natural citizens of the United States?"

One little girl replied, "Oh no, I was born Caesarean section."

———

"Daddy, are you sure Harold listens to me when I pray?"

"I don't know, honey. Who's Harold?"

"He's our heavenly Father, Dad! Remember? You taught me to pray, 'Our Father who art in heaven, Harold be thy name...'"

———

Teacher: "In this box I'm holding, I have a ten-foot snake."

Sammy: "You can't fool me, Teacher.. Snakes don't have feet."

———

Teacher: "If I had seven oranges in one hand and eight oranges in the other, what would I have?"

Jimmy: "Big hands!"

———

Teacher: "How can you prevent diseases caused by biting insects?"

Minny: "Don't bite any more insects!"

———

Teacher: "Tommy, why do you always get so dirty?"

Tommy: "Well, I'm a lot closer to the dirty ground than you are!"

———

Mother: "Why on earth did you swallow the money I gave you?"

Missy: "Because you said it was my lunch money!"

—◆—

The Do-It-Yourself Church

Is it possible that perhaps you have already heard about this "do-it-yourself church" in Burley, Idaho, because it made both local and national news? It's a church with a most interesting history. This congregation purchased an old one-room schoolhouse and prepared to move it into town and set it over a basement they would dig. Then they planned to build a foundation for it. Sounds simple, right? At least they thought so.

They had the school jacked up and on runners waiting for the basement and foundation to be completed. However when they dug down about six inches, they hit solid lava bedrock! This was in the middle of town. Much to their dismay, they discovered the porous lava rock absorbed much of the first dynamite charge. Each succeeding dynamite blast removed only small chunks. It looked like a long and laborious job.

One of the local farmers, a church member who was involved with project, said, "This will take forever. Let's tie a bunch of sticks of dynamite together and set it off in this hole." The resulting explosion shattered every window on the west side of the hospital and put some impressive-sized boulders on their roof!

Once the hole had been blasted and the foundation and basement walls were poured, they realized they had forgotten to make a hole for the water and sewer pipes. This same farmer suggested blasting a small hole in the wall with some of the leftover dynamite. To this day, nobody knows (a) why they let him talk them into the idea, or (b) just how much dynamite he used. But he blew a hole in the east wall of the newly formed basement and blew the entire north wall into the street!

Months later, the school had been turned into a church, and the job was just about completed except for painting and finishing of the basement. A special business meeting was called to decide on the options for the basement. The options were to plaster, panel, or paint. As the hours got later, tempers got shorter. Finally the "dynamite" farmer stood up and announced, "Tomorrow morning, I am sending my boys into town. If the basement is not done by then, they will paint the whole thing, upstairs and basement and outside—walls, floors, and ceilings—barn red because we've got lots of it left from painting our barns!"

The other voting members finished their coffee, went home, changed their clothes, and returned to finish the basement and paint the sanctuary. Oh by the way, at 7:00 a.m. the next morning, the job was done!

What else can we say? God works in strange ways sometimes, but God and people can get the job done!

But then again, you can't always be in charge and control the outcomes. For example, one particular day in an unnamed town (yes, the above story and this one are both true stories, so you know why they are anonymous), it happened to be a blistering, record-setting hot day. The house was full of church ladies for their monthly meeting, and things were not going too well. Finally, the hostess managed to get everyone quieted and ready for the lunch to be served. The hostess thought it would be nice and cute if her seven-year-old daughter would say the "grace" over the lunch.

"But, Mother," said the little girl, "I don't know what to say!"

"Yes, you do," said her mother. "Just say the last prayer you heard me use."

Obediently, the child bowed her head and recited quite loudly so all could hear, "Oh Lord, why in the world did I invite these fussy and demanding ladies on such a stinking, lousy, miserable day?"

"And whoever gives one of these little ones only a cup of cold water in the name of a disciple, assuredly, I say to you, he [she] shall by no means lose his [her] reward" (Matthew 10:42).

BUT SERIOUSLY FOLKS: Do you think Jesus was always joyful? Why did He laugh? Is it possible to live a joyful life in spite of circumstances over which we have no control? I think there are at least three life principles at work in His life and teaching. Thomas Chalmers answers our questions: "The grand essentials of happiness are something to love, something to do, something to hope for!" There you have them in balance—work, worship, and hope!

LET THE CATS OUT...
If you ever bought a DVD of fish in an aquarium to entertain your feline—you might be a cat lover.

The Best Is Yet To Come!

A reporter interviewed a 104-year-old woman: "And what do you think is the best thing about being 104?"

She simply replied, "No peer pressure."

A little old lady who was on her death bed called her pastor because she wanted to give him special instructions about her upcoming funeral. She was a fun-loving, wonderful old gal, the pastor thought. He sat beside her bed to listen to her request.

She said, "I'm asking you because my family refused to do this. At the final viewing, I want to be holding a fork in my hand for all to see."

A bit taken aback, he asked, "Why?"

"Easy. Whenever you are invited for a nice dinner at a friend's house who is known for her cooking, when clearing the table, she will say, 'Keep your fork,' and everybody knows what that means—dessert, saved for the last course, will be the best."

The pastor says, "I think I get your concept."

And she concluded, "The fork tells everybody that I believe the best is yet to come for me!"

The local TV news station was interviewing an eighty-four-year-old lady because she had just gotten married for the fourth time, and it had caused quite a stir.

The interviewer asked her questions about her life, about what it had felt like to be marrying again at eighty-four, and about her new husband's occupation.

"He's a funeral director," she answered.

Very interesting, the reporter thought.

Then she was asked if she would be so kind as to tell the audience a little bit about her first three husbands, who had all passed on. She paused for a few moments as she reflected on those years. With a smile she answered proudly as she explained, "My first husband was a banker, and I married him in my twenties. The second husband was a circus ringmaster, and we were in our forties and enjoyed a life of travel. Then in my sixties I married a preacher; and now in my eighties, the funeral director."

The interviewer looked at her, quite astonished, and asked, "Why did you marry four so different men with such diverse careers?"

After another long pause, she smiled and explained, "I married one for the money, two for the show, three to get ready, and four to go!"

The Dead Cow Lecture

Freshman students at the Purdue University Veterinary School were attending their first anatomy class with a real dead cow. They all gathered around the very large surgery table with the cow covered by a white sheet. The professor began the class lecture by telling them: "In veterinary medicine it is necessary to have two important qualities as a doctor. The first is that you not be disgusted by anything involving the animal's body."

For an example of this concept, the professor pulled back the sheet, stuck his finger in the mouth of the cow, withdrew it, and stuck his finger in his mouth. Then he told his students, "Go ahead and do the same thing."

Of course the students freaked out, hesitated for several minutes, and waited for the first one to follow the professor's lead. Eventually they worked up their courage and took turns sticking a finger in the mouth of the dead cow and then sucking on it.

When all had finished, the professor looked at them and said, "The second most important quality is observation. I stuck in my middle finger and sucked on my index finger.

Now learn to pay attention. Life's tough, but it's even tougher if you're stupid!"

One nice thing about being senile is that you can hide your own Easter eggs and have the fun of finding them!

An elderly lady was preparing her last will and testament. She told the preacher and the funeral director she had two final requests: "First I want to be cremated, and second, I want my ashes to be scattered over our local Walmart."

Both the men were a bit taken aback, and the preacher asked, "Why Walmart?"

"Then I'll be sure my daughters will visit me on a regular basis!"

I feel like my body has gotten totally out of shape, so I got my doctor's permission to join a local fitness club and start exercising. I began with an aerobics class for seniors. I bent, twisted, gyrated, jumped up and down, and perspired for an hour. But by the time I got my leotards on, the class was over!

A friend of mine sure has gotten old! He's had two bypass surgeries, a hip replacement, new knees, fought prostate cancer and diabetes. He's half-blind, can't hear anything quieter than a jet engine, takes forty different kinds of medications that makes him dizzy, winded, and subject to blackouts, has bouts with dementia, has poor circulation, and can hardly feel his hands and feet anymore. He can't remember if he's eighty-five or ninety-two. I asked him how he could remain so happy. He said, "Thank God, I still have my driver's license!"

—

Always remember this: You don't stop laughing because you grow old!

—

A Look Back for Those of Us Who Were Born Before 1954...

The years fly by and annually we each become a year older, a quite depressing thought until one considers the alternative. Let's share the following thought-provoking facts, before it's too late.

We were born before plasma or digital television, before penicillin, polio shots, flu shots, frozen foods, Xerox, plastic, contact lenses, Frisbees, and the Pill. We were born before radar, credit cards, debit cards, split atoms, laser beams, portable Kleenex packs, and ballpoint pens or highlighting pens for that matter. Before pantyhose, automatic dishwashers, automatic front-loading, top-loading clothes washers, clothes dryers, electric blankets, foam mattresses, select-comfort beds, air-conditioners, drip-dry clothes, no-iron clothes, and before anybody even dreamed of walking on the moon!

In our time, closets were for hanging clothes in and not coming out of. Bunnies were small rabbits, and rabbits were not Volkswagens.

We thought fast food was what you ate during Lent and outer space was the back balcony of the Galaxy theater. We were before house husbands, computer dating, dual careers, and computer marriages. We never heard of FM radio, Sirius radio, tape decks, CDs, DVDs, electric typewriters, computer keyboards, iPods, iPads, cell phones, printouts, digital everything, artificial hearts, word processors, fax machines, e-mail, Twitter, Facebook, game boxes, yogurt, and guys wearing earrings! For us, time-sharing meant togetherness...not computers or condominiums. A chip meant a piece of wood. Hardware really meant hardware, and software wasn't even a word or a concept!

Back then..."Made in Japan" meant junk, "making out" referred to how you did on your exams. Pizzas, McDonalds, Starbucks, Gucci, instant coffee, instant hot chocolate, and frozen dinners were all unheard of. We hit the scene when there were "five-and-ten-cent" stores where you actually bought things for five and ten cents, when the corner drugstore sold ice cream cones for a nickel or a dime. For a nickel you could mail a first-class letter or ride a streetcar, make a phone call, buy a Coca-Cola or a Dr. Pepper, and a candy bar or all-day sucker. You could buy a Chevy or Ford coupe for $600, but who could afford one? That was a real pity because gas was only 15 cents per gallon!

In our day grass was mowed, not smoked! Coke was a real drink and pot was something you cooked in, made soup in, or boiled corn on the cob in. Rock music was what Grandma did as she sang a lullaby to grandbabies in her rocking chair as they went to sleep.

AIDS were helpers in the principal's office. We learned to make do with what we had, and if we didn't have it and we still wanted it, we worked hard for it or made it ourselves.

We had never learned of the poverty line because all of us lived beneath it. We didn't know what food stamps were or unemployment compensation—getting paid for not working was unbelievable.

No wonder we are so confused and there is such a generation gap today, unheard of back then—what gap? But we survived!

So what better reasons do we have to celebrate?

The race is not to the swift, nor the battle to the strong, nor bread to the wise, nor riches to men of understanding, nor favor to men of skill; but time and chance happen to them all (Ecclesiastes 9:11).

BUT SERIOUSLY FOLKS: So what's new? In our world, sometimes it seems as though everything is new, but the more they change, the more they stay the same. The only way to deal with an uncertain future is to be grounded and live a joy-filled life and stay flexible. Loosely translated, then: "The flexible shall eventually inherit the earth!"

LET THE CATS OUT...
There is no snooze button on a cat who wants breakfast.

And Now for the Pun of It!

"A pun is a practical joke played upon the mind, not by means of a deceptive meaning, but by means of a flaw in the vehicle of meaning."
—*Max Eastman, Enjoyment of Laughter*

> A pun is the lowest form of wit,
> It does not tax the brain a bit;
> One merely takes a word that's plain
> And picks one out that sounds the same.
>
> Perhaps some letter may be changed
> Or others slightly disarranged,
> This to the meaning gives a twist,
> Which much delights the humorist.
>
> A sample now may help to show
> The way a good pun ought to go:
> "It isn't the cough, that carries you off,
> It's the coffin they carry you off in."
> —*Art Moger, The Complete Pun Book*

The crow perched himself on a telephone wire because he wanted to make a long distance caw.

The snake charmer wooed and won a lady undertaker. One of their most cherished wedding gifts was a set of towels, marked: "Hiss" and "Hearse."

There's the two-hundred-pound lady who always insists she's on a diet, though none has ever spotted her observing it. Her husband calls her "the wishful shrinker."

The Eskimo stabbed himself with an icicle. He died of cold cuts.

Then there is the San Antonio restaurateur whose pie list suggests, "Remember the ala-mode."

The commuter had a Volkswagen that broke down once too often. He consigned it to the "Old Volks' Home."

There was the bookseller who was dawdling over a second cup of coffee one Sunday morning, reading *The Chaucer Tales*. His wife demanded, "What have you got there?" He answered, "Just my cup and Chaucer."

The advice to the lovelorn editor who insists: "If at first you don't succeed, try a little ardor."

The Pennsylvania farmer with relatives in East Germany heard that a food package he had sent never arrived. He answered, "Cheer up! The wurst is yet to come!"

"Cheerful people," declare Dr. Wilbur Abercrombie, "resist intestinal diseases better than gloomy ones." What the doctor obviously means is that the surly bird catches the worm.

Frank Sinatra once hired a chef imported from Bombay, but after serving the same menu six nights in a row, he was fired. Explained Sinatra, "This was one poor guy who got fired for favoring curry."

They say what Christopher Columbus really told Queen Isabella when he got home from his American tour was:

"Well, I bet I'm the first man who ever got nineteen hundred miles on a galleon...."

The new bride said to her new husband: "Let's get a new sports car. I love to hear the patter of a tiny Fiat."

Sign in a small hotel: "Please turn off the lights when not using them. Thanks a watt!"

Did you hear about the gal who, when she heard that her boyfriend's car needed a new muffler, started to knit one for him?   —*Harry Trigg, WGN-TV*

Harry O. Kinsman swears he saw a bumper sticker that read: "Support your right to arm bears."

Cavewoman to her caveman husband: "Don't just stand there—slay something!"

Laughter as Medicine...Is Really No Joke!

The Reverend Oscar Johnson, a jovial former St. Louis clergyman, told this one on himself: "Once after a change of churches, I met a woman from my former flock, and asked her, 'How do you like your new pastor?'"

"Just fine," she beamed. "But somehow or other, he just doesn't seem to hold me like you did."

Dr. Bernie S. Siegel, a mind-body health guru, prescribes

the healing power of humor like this: "The writer Balzac called life, with all of its tragedies and twists, a human comedy. There is a lot in life that seems unfair, but seeing the absurdity, finding something to laugh at, makes it easier to endure and certainly a lot more fun. It also combats illness!"

Dr. Siegel goes on: "For instance, I knew this man who was in the hospital for a bone-marrow transplant. He was a real character. One day, he was lying in his room and over-heard his doctor tell his wife in jest, 'You know, what your husband really needs is a brain transplant'!"

Interestingly enough, what the doctor said made this man laugh because he felt not like a cancer patient, but like a real person. Okay...a crazy person, but a person! A person who, no matter what life handed him, had the power to make himself and others laugh. What's more, this particular man left the hospital in less than half the time this medical procedure warranted. In fact, some of the other patients waiting or re-covering from a transplant were thinking, *Maybe we should act a little crazy, too. If we were fun loving characters, we'd be on our feet quicker, too.*

There are myriads more of examples of humor helping the healing process: One lady, on the morning before abdom-inal surgery, had painted her stomach with cartoons so that when the covers were drawn back, the medical staff was pre-sented with a real work of art!

Another cancer patient wore "Groucho Marx" glasses with the huge nose every time she went to see her doctor!

One man, undergoing chemotherapy, announced for all to hear that he was saving his hair that was falling out so he could make a pet!

Such people are survivors! Laughter is really the best kind of medicine. Remember that the Bible says, "A cheerful heart is good medicine" (Proverbs 17:22 NIV).

Laughing is like a good aerobic workout! According to Dr. William Fry, associate clinical professor at Stanford University, "Laughing 100 times a day gives the same boost to your heart and lungs as ten minutes of hard rowing. Tickling the funny bone causes the body to release natural painkillers, and a good laugh will give you two hours of pain relief! Laughing also releases and mobilizes infection-fighting antibodies. It decreases blood levels of stress hormones such as adrenaline and cortisol so that we are more disease resistant! Laughter is the pulse of life!"

Then there was the veteran missionary who was assigned the following subject to speak about in a conference: "What I Would Pack in My Suitcase IF I Were to Return to the Mission Field." You guessed it...it was a very short message and the first item on her list, she pointedly said, was "a sense of humor!"

Another missionary at this same conference expressed it like this: "You really need two things if you want to be happy in God's work overseas: a good sense of humor and no sense of smell!"

One more time, I remind you: You don't stop laughing just because you grow old!

A merry heart makes a cheerful countenance, but by sorrow of the heart the spirit is broken (Proverbs 15:13).

BUT SERIOUSLY FOLKS: Did you happen to pick up on the health benefits of laughter that Dr. Siegel outlined? Perhaps you need to read this again. There are psychological benefits to laughter—it extinguishes body tensions, gives us a boost, and reduces stress. The cardiovascular benefits include decreased blood pressure, lowered heart rates, and enhanced circulation. The muscular benefits include a strengthening of the heart muscles; it also relaxes the muscles throughout the body and helps to move nutrients and oxygen to body tissues. Awesome! Laugh your way to better health! A laugh a day keeps the doctor away!

LET THE CATS OUT...
If there are no human beings in your photo album—you might be a cat lover.

A Few "Zingers" (one-liners) To Make Your Day Brighter

- Can you really afford to give anybody a "piece" of your mind?

- If they can put one man on the moon, why not all of them?

- Shin: a sensitive device for finding furniture in the dark.

- Don't eat onions and beans at the same time—you'll get tear gas.

- If at first you don't succeed, then skydiving is probably not for you.

- The helpline for frazzled mothers is 1-800-G-R-A-N-D-M-A!

- If it weren't for electricity, we'd all be watching television by candlelight.

- All you really have to do if you want the world to beat a path to your door is take a nap.

- Is it because light travels faster than sound that people appear bright until they speak?

- The difference between a professor and a terrorist is that you can negotiate with a terrorist.

- Did you hear about the teacher who retired and lost all her principals?

- A class reunion is where people get together to see who's falling apart.

- The trouble with giving advice is that people want to repay you.

- It's good to let your mind go blank occasionally, but only if you turn the sound off.

- We don't like people who won't admit their faults because we would if we had any.

- There are three faithful friends...an old wife, an old dog, and your power chair.

- I'm so old that when I was born, the Dead Sea wasn't even sick.

- Every day above ground is a good day.

- If you are yearning for the good old days, just turn off your air-conditioner.

- He is a new high-tech ventriloquist. He can throw his voice mail.

- If the funeral procession is at night, do folks drive with their headlights off?

- Old preachers never retire, they just go out to pastor.

- We could quickly wipe out the national debt if there was a tax on campaign promises.

- One party can't fool all the people all the time. That's why we have two parties.

- One lawyer to another, "I believe a person is innocent until they run out of money."

- It's been so dry this year in the Ozarks that the trees are following the dogs around.

BUT SERIOUSLY FOLKS: Laughter is joy overflowing. It's happiness showing. It's a countenance-glowing kind of an attitude. Arm yourself with an attitude that is disciplined to express love and joyfulness in all kinds of human experiences. Try it! It can literally change your relationships for the better!

LET THE CATS OUT...
God created dogs to love man. He created cats to teach him humility.

The Church Is Still a Very Funny Place

(The following are all true stories involving real people, no joke.)

An Episcopalian priest was talking with me at a ministers' meeting and telling me of a conversation he'd had with a charismatic lady from his parish about a local faith-healing revival that she had recently attended. The lady enthused, "Then he healed a man suffering from constipation with a single word of command!"

The priest looked at me with a smile and said, "I suppose I shall always wonder which particular word he used."

~

A. W. Tozer wrote: "A real Christian is an odd number anyway. He feels supreme love for One whom he has never seen, talks familiarly every day to Someone he cannot see, expects to go to heaven on the virtue of Another, empties himself in order to be full, admits he is wrong so he can be declared right, goes down in order to get up, is strongest when he is worst. He dies so he can live, forsakes in order to have, gives away so he can keep, sees the invisible, hears the inaudible, and knows that which passes knowledge."

~

Pastor William Goodin recalls: "One of the wildest, most fun-loving congregations I have had the privilege of serving was a small church in Washington state. During our ministry there, they had an 'ugly baby' contest; a General George Custer memorial ice cream feast on the date Custer was "creamed" at Little Big Horn; a Joan of Arc memorial barbecue on the date Joan was burned at the stake; a party door prize that was an actual door; piñatas filled with warm peanut butter (and you can't begin to imagine the mess from that one); and "musical onion," where the potent veggie is passed around and then must be eaten by the holder (er, victim) when the music stops. After seven years with that wild bunch, I started to fear that I would not know how to minister to 'normal' people!"

Is Billy Dawson a typical church member? Well, let's find out. Billy was sitting in his house during a torrential downpour. Soon the floodwaters from a nearby creek reached the bottom of his front door, and some friends came along in a rowboat and called to him to climb in. But Billy said, "No, I'm trusting the Lord for deliverance. I'll be okay. I'm staying here."

The rain kept coming down and the floodwaters kept rising until Billy took refuge on the second floor. A police rescue boat came by, and Billy again said, "I'm trusting in the Lord, and I'm staying until He helps me." The waters kept rising, and soon he was sitting on his roof. A helicopter hovered overhead, dropped down a rope, and shouted for Billy to climb aboard. "No, I'm trusting in the Lord and I'm staying here."

The rains kept coming and the floodwaters continued

rising until old Billy finally drowned. Arriving in heaven, Bill said to the Lord, "Lord, I just don't understand it. I trusted completely in You, and I still ended up dead, drowned."

And the Lord replied, "Well, Billy, I don't understand it either. First I sent you a boat, then another boat. And finally I sent you a helicopter, but you didn't take any of them!"

———

There was a small Kentucky town that had two churches and one whiskey distillery. Members of both churches complained that the distillery gave the town a bad image, and it was a bad example for kids. On top of this, the owner of the distillery was an atheist. They had tried to shut down the place but were unsuccessful. At last, the churches decided to hold a joint prayer meeting to ask the Lord to intervene and shut the place down.

Saturday night came, and all through the prayer meeting a raging electrical storm lit up the sky with lightning. To the delight of the church members, lightning struck the distillery and it burned to the ground as they watched and gave God praise. The following Sunday morning, sermons in both churches were about the power of prayer.

Fire insurance adjusters promptly notified the distillery owner they would not pay for his damages because the fire was caused by an "act of God," and such acts were not covered in his policy.

Whereupon the distillery owner sued all the church members, claiming they had conspired with God to destroy his business. The defendants denied absolutely that they had done anything to cause the fire! The judge observed, "I find more than one thing about this case perplexing. We have a plaintiff who is an atheist, professing his belief in the power of God and prayer, and the defendants, good church members, who are denying the power of God and prayer!"

I thank my God upon every remembrance of you, always in every prayer of mine making request for you all with joy, for your fellowship... (Philippians 1:3–5).

A special speaker was to arrive barely in time to make it to church on a Sunday morning visit. The pastor was busy with the church service and preparations, so he sent the head deacon to the airport to greet the guest and bring him to church. The deacon had a poor memory for names so the pastor, knowing the problem, said, "The man's name is Reverend Ben Acker." Thinking word association would help the deacon's poor memory, he continued, "What do you do with an 'ack?" You apply linament. Linament...acker. Got it? Reverend Ben Acker."

So the deacon greeted the distinguished guest at the airport with: "Welcome, Brother Ben Gay!"

Dr. Charles Swindoll, well-known preacher and writer, confessed to getting his tongue twisted up more than once. But perhaps the most exciting time happened as he was describing the unusual strategy Joshua and his army used to bring down the walls of Jericho. Swindoll tells us, "Instead of saying they were to march around the wall, I chose to say that they 'circumscribed' the wall, but inadvertently it came out, they 'circumcised' the wall, which brought the house down. You're very ready to pronounce the benediction after a blooper like that!"

Reverend James Beall of Detroit's Bethesda Christian Church brought his crowd to attention with the following announcement: "Friends, our church's softball team is on a winning streak. We're undefeated. Our problem is small crowds. As pastor I want to urge you to join Mrs. Beall and myself this Friday night at the ball park. Let's cheer our team on to victory. We all can't be athletes, but we should all be athletic supporters!"

Pastor Goodin recalls a most memorable ice cream social and cake auction at their church, which was to raise money for a special youth ministry project. At one point the bidding for a beautifully decorated cake was up to $26 and still going hot and heavy. The chief bidder finally asked, "WHO is bidding against me?"

The auctioneer answered, "Nobody...why?"

And at the same event, just a bit later in the cake auction, a cherry-covered cheesecake was going for a final bid of $15. From the back of the room a voice called out, "I'll give you thirty dollars for it if you will put it in Paul's face." (Paul was chairman of the church board.)

The auctioneer looked around, saw Paul standing behind him...not paying attention to the proceedings...and quickly said, "Thirty dollars! Once, twice, going, going, going... (whap!)...and gone!"

There stood our esteemed chairman of the board looking rather surprised and very nicely covered with cherries and cheesecake!

Humor and laughter, used at the right moment, can save just about any difficult or embarrassing social occasion! A good laugh in time, how sweet it is. A good laugh is therapy at work when nothing else does the trick!

Laughter and joyfulness are first attitudes and then they become actions. Attitudes are formed by convictions. People who have developed strong convictions as to who they are, where they are going, who God is in their lives, what His love is about, and what His Word says about joy, have healthier attitudes toward life than those who do not have such deep-seated convictions!

"Forgiving one another, if anyone has a complaint against another; even as Christ forgave you, so you also must do. But above all these things put on love, which is the bond of perfection" (Colossians 3:13–14).

BUT SERIOUSLY FOLKS: Dr. Siegel wrote: "Humor is one of the strongest bonds between people!" Therefore, the church that laughs together lasts together. The apostle Paul fondly remembers the church in Philippi with joy! What a way to live! Laugh with people you worship with and experience no regrets, no nursed bitter feelings, and no unresolved conflicts. When Paul remembered, he did it with a smile, a laugh, and much joy! Positive, happy, joyful memories make life so much fuller and the burdens of life much lighter. How about renaming your church the Church of the Good Laugh?

LET THE CATS OUT...

If you get all teary-eyed when Felix leaves for a week of obedience school—you might be an unrealistically optimistic cat lover.

Ever Have an Accident,
Make a Mistake, or Misspeak?

A small country church was having a "baptizing" in a river on a cold January day. The revival meeting had just concluded. The preacher asked one candidate, "Is the water cold?"

"Naw..." he replied.

One of the deacons, standing nearby, shouted, "Dip him agin', Preacher, he's still lyin'!"

One particular airlines company was disturbed over the high percentage of accidents and decided to eliminate all human errors by building a completely computerized, hi-tech mechanical airplane.

On the maiden voyage, a voice came over the loudspeakers in the plane: "Ladies and gentlemen, it may interest you to know that you are now traveling in the world's first completely automatic plane. We have eliminated human error as the computer will fly this plane with no human pilots on board. Now sit back and relax because your flight will be totally trouble free...totally trouble free...totally trouble free...totally trouble free..."

The truck driver of the automobile transport had his

truck headlights go out, so he stopped the truck, climbed up, and turned the lights of the top car on, then climbed into the cab of his truck and continued. An approaching car veered sharply and drove off the highway. Alarmed, the truck driver stopped and ran back to help. "What made you drive into the ditch?" he asked.

"Well," he replied. "I thought if you were as wide as you were high, I would never get by."

—

Lady Motorist: "I'm sorry. I'm afraid this accident was largely my fault."

Gentleman Driver: "Nonsense! The blame rests entirely with me. I saw you at least three blocks away and had plenty of time to swerve down a side street."

—

Former Governor Al Smith, soon after he'd been elected governor of New York, visited Sing Sing Prison. He was asked to have lunch and afterwards say a few words to the prisoners. He cleared his throat and began, "Fellow Democrats..." but quickly caught himself, knowing no good Democrat should be in prison.

He started again, "Fellow citizens..." but caught himself again, knowing that criminals often lost their citizenship.

He backed up for the third attempt and said, "My friends...I'm glad to see you all here!"

—

Fred Abernathy always read the obituary column of the morning paper, first thing. All of his friends knew of his habit, so one day they decided to play a trick on him. The next morning Fred picked up his paper, turned to the obit page, and there he was, photo, name, and bio.

Startled, he phoned his pal, George. "Listen," he said. "Do you have the morning paper? You do? Turn to the obit page... You have? What do you see in the second column?"

There was a long pause, then George said, "Holy smoke! That's you, Fred! Yes, that's really you! Listen...by the way, just where are you calling from?"

⎯◄

A CEO boarded the New York to Chicago overnight train. He carefully explained to the porter, "I'm a heavy sleeper, and I want you to be sure and wake me at 3:00 a.m. to get me off in Buffalo. Regardless of what I say or do, get me up and get me off the train because I have some very important business in Buffalo."

The next morning he awakened in Chicago and was he steaming! He found the porter and really poured it on with abusive language. After he had finished his tirade and stomped off, still mad as a wet hen, another passenger had overheard and asked the porter, "How could you stand there and take that kind of talk from that man?"

The porter replied, "That ain't nothing. You should have heard what the man said that I threw off in Buffalo."

⎯◄

"Our cleaning lady has stolen two of our bath towels. Crook!" shouted the wife.

"Which towels, dear?" her husband asked.

"You know," she replied, "those really nice ones from that fancy hotel in Miami."

An elderly lady had a parrot that used offensive language and among other things told her, "I wish you were dead."

She complained to her pastor, and he said, "We too have a parrot, but it's never rude or offensive. You just bring your parrot to spend a couple of weeks with our parrot and maybe my parrot's good behavior might rub off."

So she did. Returning after two weeks, as she opened the door and walked in, her parrot said: "I wish you were dead!"

The pastor's parrot chimed in and said, "Amen! Praise the Lord and grant her spoken request!"

Tithing and a Little More

A man scheduled an appointment with his pastor to deal with a specific issue. The time arrived and the member said, "I really want to tithe, I want to give ten percent of my income to my church, but there's a problem."

The pastor nodded. "What seems to be the problem?"

"When my income was fifty dollars a week, I regularly gave five every Sunday. Then I became a businessman with my own business and my income rose to five hundred dollars a week and I gave fifty dollars per week. But now my income has grown to five thousand dollars a week and I just can't seem to bring myself to write a five-hundred-dollar check to the church each Sunday."

The pastor said, "Why don't we pray about this?"

The businessman lowered his head as the pastor prayed: "Dear God, you have heard this man's plea. Please answer his prayer and return this man's weekly income to five hundred dollars a week so he can be a faithful tither. Amen!"

James R. Swanson, of Costa Mesa, has proposed a simple plan that he says will solve the financial problems of all churches, enabling them to increase pastors' salaries, pay off church mortgages, eliminate all other fundraisers, build new churches, and allow greater missions work and more.

Swanson calls it the Flat Tithe Plan: Every Christian, regardless of income, would simply give the church a flat 10 percent of his or her earnings. This would be treated as a withholding from the weekly paycheck and paid directly into the church's checking account. Nothing to it; simple, easy to figure, and easy to give.

He then concludes, "I wonder why someone hasn't thought of this before?"

I could not resist making the pun: "It Costa Mesa money to run a church these days!"

A kid moved to El Paso from Dallas, and at their new church, pledged $200 a week to their Methodist church. The pastor thought this ten-year-old didn't understand or was making a joke or fooling around with a pledge card, so he called the boy's father and told him about the pledge the kid had signed.

"That's quite all right," the father said. "We believe firmly that Johnny should tithe his weekly income. He's in oil, you know!"

An elderly miser, because of his exceptional thrift, had no

friends. Just before he died, he called his doctor, lawyer, and minister to his bedside. "I have always heard it said that you can't take it with you, but I have no friends or family to leave it with, so I am going to prove you can take it with you!" He continued, "I have nine hundred thousand dollars in cash under my mattress. It's equally divided into three packages of three hundred thousand dollars each. When I pass on, I want each of you to take a package, and just before they close the casket for the last time, as you pass by, toss your package into my casket."

After he died, the three attended his graveside funeral, and sure enough, each threw his envelope into the casket. Riding together in the same funeral car after the graveside service, the minister finally blurted out, "I just don't feel exactly right. I badly needed some money for our new addition, so I took out a hundred thousand dollars and threw the two hundred thousand dollars into the casket."

Then the doctor said, "I also need to confess. I'm building a new office building and needed financial help, so I kept two hundred thousand dollars, and threw in only one hundred thousand!"

The lawyer said, "Gentlemen, gentlemen, I'm surprised, shocked, and embarrassed to call you my friends. I don't see how you could hold out like this on the old man. I threw in my personal check for the full amount of three hundred thousand dollars!"

A well-heeled tourist dropped in to a tiny village church in Essex County, England. Before it began, he buttonholed the rector and said proudly, "I plan to give you a handsome contribution. I only hope you'll put on a good show today."

The rector answered quietly, "It won't be a bad one. This show's been running now for about two thousand years."

There was a time when a fool and his money were soon parted...but now, it happens to everybody!

A rural pastor peeked in the collection plate and spied three nickels. "Ahem," he said, "I perceive a tightwad in our midst today."

"Oh, Reverend," came a small voice from a back pew. "There's three of us."

The church was in desperate need of money and the pastor began calling on members in private. One member bluntly refused to contribute one dollar more than his regular offering. "Don't you feel you owe the Lord something more?" the pastor asked.

"Certainly," the man replied, "but He isn't pushing me the way some of my other creditors are doing."

An IRS agent phoned a minister and said, "I'm auditing the tax returns of one of your church members, a Mr. McPherson, who lists a donation of $26,000 to your church. Can you tell me if he actually made this contribution?"

The minister replied, "Well, I'll have to check with our church treasurer...but if he didn't, he will!"

A father wanted to develop his son's character, so he gave him a dollar bill and a five dollar bill as they entered the church. "Put one in the collection plate," he told his son.

After church he asked the son which bill he had given. "I gave the one dollar," the boy explained because, "just before they passed the plates, the preacher said, 'The Lord loves a cheerful giver.' I knew I could be more cheerful if I gave the dollar, so that's what I did."

Speaking of money and the super rich, the Chartis Insurance Company swears the following insurance claim is true: A $50 million-plus painting fell off the wall onto a $4 million, eighteenth-century chest of drawers, cracking the marble top. As the painting fell, it knocked a $6 million Rodin bronze and a pair of eighteenth-century porcelain candelabra onto the floor. The arm of the Rodin broke off, piercing a $1 million carpet and denting the floor beneath! Lesson: if you are rich, make sure you position your expensive stuff more wisely!

The owner of a 2005 Bentley Continental ($380,000 new) was unable to start the car after not driving it for months. But with an alternative battery he managed to get it started and parked it in his driveway. He figured the fastest way to charge the battery would be to keep the engine running at a high RPM. To do this, he put a brick on the gas pedal, which would rev the engine to its redline limits. He left it like that to take a shower. When he returned twenty minutes later, the overheated engine had seized, melted, stuck, and hot oil was spewing everywhere! The car was totaled while sitting in the driveway!

The pastor's son applied to become a policeman. During

his oral examination he was asked, "How would you scatter a mob that is protesting?"

Quickly, he replied, "I'd take off my hat and start taking up a collection."

—

The preacher was going over the order of service for the worship band: "And when I get through with my sermon, which will be about giving, I'll end with an appeal to the congregation about who would like to give at least fifty dollars to the building fund to please stand. At this time, you will play the appropriate music."

"What do you mean, 'appropriate' music?" asked the worship leader.

" 'The Star-Spangled Banner,' of course!"

—

A young lady enthusiastically described her new boyfriend to her father. "He sounds quite nice, dear," said her dad, "but does he have any money and a job?"

She replied, "Oh, you men are all alike. He asked me the same thing about you."

—

Then there was the optimist who said, "I don't worry because I have enough money to last me the rest of my life...unless I buy something!"

—

LET THE CATS OUT...

If you wait at the kitty litter box with scoop in hand, anticipating its next use—you might be a cat lover.

Finally, if you go to let the cat out and you inadvertently let Fido out too—you might be an absent-minded cat lover.